Fearless Leadership

All management starts with self-management – handle fear and become an authentic leader. Often, the problem with management is not theoretical, but practical. Managers know enough about leadership, but a lot of them do not act accordingly. They know what should be done in a given situation but fear the discomfort and uncertainty that comes with it.

The fear keeps many managers from stepping up to their responsibility. Therefore, the fear in leadership is playing a decisive role in the life and effectiveness of organisations. Based on research on the theoretical knowledge and the practical behaviour of managers, combined with a long-time experience as consultants, the authors argue for the importance of practical judgement and emotional courage in management. This is essential in acting as an authentic leader, who does not feel paralysed and trapped in paradoxes. Management books typically address the question of "what is good management," whereas this book is concerned with how to practice good management by exercising fearless leadership and emotional courage.

It is a practical book that aims at inspiring the reader to act by providing specific tools and methods and will be of value to researchers, academics, practitioners, and students in the fields of leadership, strategic management, organisational studies, and behaviour, management development, and industrial and organisational psychology.

Morten Novrup Henriksen is a business psychologist, author and speaker in leadership. Morten is an approved specialist (postgraduate) in business psychology. He is co-creator and partner in the business psychological consultancy firm, IMPAQ, Denmark.

Thomas Lundby is a business psychologist, author and speaker in leadership. Thomas is an approved specialist (postgraduate) in business psychology. He is co-creator and partner in the business psychological consultancy firm, IMPAQ, Denmark.

Routledge Focus on Business and Management

The fields of business and management have grown exponentially as areas of research and education. This growth presents challenges for readers trying to keep up with the latest important insights. *Routledge Focus on Business and Management* presents small books on big topics and how they intersect with the world of business research.

Individually, each title in the series provides coverage of a key academic topic, whilst collectively, the series forms a comprehensive collection across the business disciplines.

Rethinking Organizational Culture
Redeeming Culture through Stories
David Collins

Management in the Non-Profit Sector
A Necessary Balance between Values, Responsibility and Accountability
Renato Civitillo

Fearless Leadership
Managing Fear, Leading with Courage and Strengthening Authenticity
Morten Novrup Henriksen and Thomas Lundby

Clusters, Digital Transformation and Regional Development in Germany
Marta Götz

Gender Bias in Organisations
From the Arts to Individualised Coaching
Gillian Danby and Malgorzata Ciesielska

For more information about this series, please visit: www.routledge.com/Routledge-Focus-on-Business-and-Management/book-series/FBM

Fearless Leadership
Managing Fear, Leading with
Courage and Strengthening
Authenticity

**Morten Novrup Henriksen
and Thomas Lundby**

Routledge
Taylor & Francis Group

NEW YORK AND LONDON

First published 2021
by Routledge
605 Third Avenue, New York, NY 10158

and by Routledge
2 Park Square, Milton Park, Abingdon, Oxon OX14 4RN

Routledge is an imprint of the Taylor & Francis Group, an informa business

Library of Congress Cataloging-in-Publication Data
A catalog record for this title has been requested

ISBN: 978-0-367-35915-7 (hbk)
ISBN: 978-1-032-02365-6 (pbk)
ISBN: 978-0-429-34259-2 (ebk)

Typeset in Times New Roman
by Newgen Publishing UK

Contents

Foreword

Never before were leaders so highly educated and never so knowledge-able about leadership. And never before have we witnessed such all-encompassing investment in leadership education.

Nonetheless, we are facing a global leadership crisis. Workplace commitment has gone into tailspin. Stress-related cases are soaring. The feeling of meaningfulness is on the wane. The majority of leaders consider themselves to be inspirational and good role models – to which very few employees can relate.

Why this gap between leadership education and relevant leadership behaviour? One very substantial explanation, discussed in this book, is the overlooked fact that the origin of all leadership is self-management. All other things being equal, a leader who is incapable of managing himself, his thoughts, his emotions, and his attentiveness will find it difficult to be a good leader of others. The authors of this book in particular demonstrate how, quite clearly defined, it is the fear of leaders that will prevent them from doing what, in most cases, they know should be done. This may be fear of coming across as steamrollering, incompetent, or weak. As long as leaders dare not confront such fears and experience the discomfort which many leadership circumstances may entail, they will not be found among those courageous leaders who actually lead, who actually take on the personal and relational leadership responsibility that is so incredibly decisive.

This is a practical book aimed at helping practicing managers bridge the knowing-doing gap in their own performance by coming to terms with fears, worries, and concerns that are presumed to hold them back from taking the sort of action that will enhance organisational performance and advance the mission but may come at some (real or perceived) personal cost. The aim of the book is to familiarise managers/leaders about their personal barriers and to 'force' them out of their comfort zone in order to become better leaders.

This is a book that, refreshingly and courageously, argues that we should stop 'pretending' and instead trust our practical judgment and say things as they are. Leaders need to take on the responsibility of leadership, take emotions seriously, work towards conquering their fears, and have the courage to assert themselves as authentic leaders and be role models to their employees.

With reference to leadership research and organisational psychology and by the many concrete examples gathered by the authors in the course of their many years as consultants and teachers within the field, the reader will be convinced of the importance of emotional courage in leadership.

It is a book that is intended for reading as well as doing. The reader will, at one and the same time, become wiser and get tools for application in the conquering of those demons that prevent the leader from asserting himself/herself as a fearless leader.

Rob Kaiser

Introduction

It is easy enough to read about leadership, learning the theories. But it is another matter when it comes to practising – when it comes to finding the right words and pluck up the courage to risk going through the discomfort and uncertainty of speaking up. In a nutshell, the crucial challenge of leadership is the challenge of emotional courage (Bregman, 2013).

You *know* enough about leadership. But something prevents you from *being* a leader. Never before were there so many leadership development programmes. Never before have leaders known so much about leadership and leadership theories. But why then, will the leader frequently shy away from addressing adverse behaviour and conflicts? From setting the course? From pouncing upon poor quality? From insisting on collaboration? And from speaking his/her mind in the management group?

In our capacity as business psychologists we have, for many years, been occupied with organisational and management development. And, for a number of years, we have been external lecturers in Master Programmes at the University of Southern Denmark and Copenhagen Business School. Our work has demonstrated that, rather than being theoretical, the problem is frequently a practical one. Most leaders have sufficient knowledge about management and leadership. They seldom act on this knowledge, however. We have seen – and still see – leaders participating in courses at which their minds get crammed with the extents to which they need to create zest for work, work out strategies, lead the way, demonstrate energy, be visionary, cope with conflicts, etc. And we have seen – and still see – them return to their organisations and more or less continue doing what they have always done.

Our observations made us curious about understanding the background for this gap between knowledge and action. Hence, we set out to investigate the phenomenon. We thus began by systematically recording leaders' responses and comments relative to what, in their experience, would keep them back from taking such action as, in fact, they knew they should; or why they would act in certain ways when, on reflection, they knew full well that this would be inexpedient. We also discussed this gap with the heads of department at the master's degree programmes. The result of our recordings and observations was surprising in the sense that it leaves no typical coherence with our perception as to who leaders are and what they represent. Leaders are ambitious, resourceful, self-assured. So, what was the problem? The answer was fear. When, as humans, we refrain from taking action on the basis of our good judgement, this is owing to our reluctance to find ourselves in such a state of discomfort and uncertainty as is related thereto. Fear is what prevents leaders from standing forth to take responsibility – from coping with such matters as will shatter the culture and lower quality. It is a kind of experience avoidance in which one tends to ignore or avoid one's internal experiences in the nature of emotions, perceptions, thoughts, etc. For this reason, we are apt to circumnavigate situations that might release such experiences. Thus, fear in management plays a decisive role in the life and effectiveness of an organisation.

In 2011, 500 leaders were asked about what they feared the most (Buch-Hansen, 2011). The answers were, in the order given:

1   Making decisions at an insecure foundation
2   Terminating employees
3   Appearing insensitive and power-crazed
4   Criticising employees
5   Being exposed as ignorant

These are highly recognisable and interesting responses. In the following chapters (Chapter 2 in particular), we shall return to the causes of fear in leadership and to a number of such predominant consequences as are entailed by fear in leadership.

Certain causes of fear will be found in the considerable complexity that is characteristic of many workplaces and in the fact that leadership roles are frequently quite fluid. Moreover, leadership teams are not designed for coping with this – neither with the complexity nor with the fluid boundaries. However, a substantial part of the answer will be found in far more basic circumstances, namely in fundamental interpersonal human needs and in various types of fear.

As a catalyst for understanding these types of fear, we found the mindset of Will Schutz' (2005) theory on The Human Element (also known as the FIRO theory (Fundamental Interpersonal Relations Orientation)) to be a very helpful instrument. This theory about the fundamental interpersonal ways in which human beings relate to each other came about on the basis of considerable research and practice. We have, ourselves, applied this mindset together with numerous leaders who all profited greatly from this method of obtaining an understanding of themselves and their behaviour. In many ways, the mindset therefore

FIRO/The Human Element®-theory

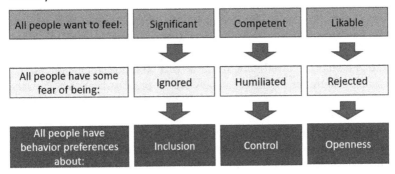

Figure 0.1 FIRO/The Human Element® theory. Basic interpersonal needs (comprising fear and behaviour). (Tamm & Luyet 2004). "Box 7–2: FIRO Theory: Feelings, Fears, and Behavior" (adapted) from *Radical Collaboration* by James W. Tamm, Ronald J. Luyet. Copyright © 2004 by James W. Tamm. Used by permission of HarperCollins Publishers.

constitutes the underlying basis for the book, illustrating its importance in leadership. Let's present a brief introduction to the theory:

Will Schutz worked with three relation themes:

- Our contact with other people (inclusion)
- Our propensity to take control, lead, and take responsibility (control)
- Our degree of confidentiality and openness (openness)

According to Schutz, one part of our behaviour concerning these themes is controlled by our preferences for certain types of behaviour and our universally human need to feel significant, competent, and likeable. Another part of our behaviour is controlled by defence mechanisms that are ascribable to our fear of feeling ignored, humiliated, and rejected. An illustration of this coherence is encapsulated by Figure 0.1:

The fear of being ignored is linked with the universally human need to feel important and to belong. Linked with the need to feel important, the fear of being ignored will have an impact on how a person will act relative to inclusion in the community. The exact situation in which an individual will be too affected by the fear of being ignored can either entail an extent of inclusion and involvement that is much too high or much too low. This may for instance release too much talk and frequent repetitions. 'I want people to listen to my opinion' Or one may refrain from taking contact and speak one's mind, thus avoiding exposure to the risk of being ignored by others.

The fear of being humiliated is linked with the universally human need to feel competent. The fear of humiliation may represent a ubiquitous presence within an organisation. Chris Argyris, one of the grand old men within organisational psychology, stated that: "Whenever human beings are faced with any issue that contains significant embarrassment or threat, they act in ways that bypass, as best they can, the embarrassment or threat." (Argyris, 1990, p. 25). According to Schutz, an individual may act more or less controllingly for the purpose of feeling competent. This is to say that the individual may thus exert more or less influence and attempt to exercise a higher or lesser extent of influence. Some leaders will cope with their fear of humiliation by exercising an all-encompassing control. Such leaders will exercise micromanagement. Others will shirk responsibility as, this way, they will not get into any tight corners.

The fear of rejection is linked with the need to feel popular/be likeable. At the very point where the fear becomes too overwhelming by far, we may be at risk of exposing ourselves and our feelings or confidential topics by revealing far too much in our attempt to keep people close. In the alternative, we may become distanced and impersonal for the purpose of protecting ourselves.

Fear has tangible and substantial consequences. Our lectures at management educations frequently embark on considerations of such consequences by introducing an exercise designed by Will Schutz, which is called 'I pretend... .' The objective of this exercise is to be investigative and curious about all those things that we humans will make pretence of in our everyday lives, typically because we fear our own reactions or those of others. The statements listed below are the most recurrent examples for leaders who carry out this exercise. Perhaps, you recognise a few?

- 'I pretend to consider my staff to be adequate and qualified.'
- 'I pretend to be in control of my department.'
- 'I pretend to consider my leader competent and capable.'
- 'I pretend not to be seriously annoyed with my staff.'
- 'I pretend to be confident at meetings.'
- 'I pretend to be indifferent about being in close proximity to my superior.'
- 'I pretend to be capable of coping with the many assignments.'
- 'I pretend that feedback is of any use to me.'
- 'I pretend not to feel really nervous or uncertain when the staff satisfaction survey is published.'

- 'I pretend to remain calm when my staff members are arguing.'
- 'I pretend to have a good grip on the strategy.'
- 'I pretend not to be tremendously upset when being criticised.'
- 'I pretend to be competent.'
- 'I pretend to be OK with my absence from family and friends.'
- 'I pretend to be in control of my department at management meetings.'

At first, there is much laughter when leaders relate about some of their 'I pretend' experiences. Very soon, however, the gravity of the situation comes through – spreading a decidedly gloomy atmosphere among the participants. Suddenly, they are in contact with themselves – with their psychological mechanisms and behavioural patterns. Suddenly, they become aware of how much they are hiding and steering clear of in their daily lives as leaders; and hence what they *fail* to cope with – and hence their contribution in respect of the creation of certain impacts. Not speaking one's mind will entail immense losses. In his research work, Will Schutz (2005) observed the work processes and communication pertaining to selected teams. One of the most obvious observations constituted the inability to speak the truth and the costs related thereto:

> People spent (and wasted) an overwhelming amount of time of not telling the truth. They were devoting energy to deciding to lie, figuring out how to present the lies, remembering what not to say and what subjects not to discuss, trying to figure out other people's lies, avoiding situations where lies might be revealed, and reconstructing the surrounding situations to make lies plausible. (…) not telling the truth is a tremendous drain on productivity.
>
> (Schutz, 2005, p. 9)

Clear Speech – Without Fear

In ancient Greece, they used the expression *parrhesia*, which means to say everything. You conceal nothing. You speak candidly. When engaging in parrhesia, you do not shroud your actual opinions in alternative terms and discourse that are, perhaps, more legitimate. You do not disguise your personal attitude (Foucault, 1999). In spite of the risk of the potential repercussions involved in telling your good friend or colleague that you believe he or she is making a mistake; in telling your employee that his/her work is not up to scratch; in telling your boss that he or she is making a poor decision. This virtue has been undermined by the predominant consideration-festered democratic discourse and perspectivism of the contemporary scene. The fact that no one can claim to have a patent on truth is turned into a practice of not being entitled to speak one's mind.

You are attending a meeting and experience that your employees are talking at cross purposes. There are too many quarrels over trifles. But you refrain from stating the obvious.[1] Instead, you subsequently grumble about your stupid staff before a circle of peer leaders or in the company of your spouse.

You are attending a meeting in your leadership team. Your leader completely fails to preside over the meeting, and you experience everyone else to be saving their own bacon. Yet, you do not speak up. The meeting leaves you angry and frustrated. Nonetheless you stick to your usual routines.

Such decision paralysis and failure to sound the alarm hamper our organisations. Too many leaders are simply sitting on the fence, failing to take responsibility, make decisions, and lead the way. Parrhesia emphasises the importance of our duty to have the courage of our convictions and to criticise where we believe criticism to be due – rather than repress such criticism, sitting on the fence.

In parrhesia, the speaker speaks his mind, rather than observing the falsehood of silence. He criticises rather than using flattery, and, not mincing his words, he puts own security and self-interest on the line. In short he meets his moral duty rather than indulging in moral apathy (Foucault, 1999, p. 6).

Alas, parrhesia is not a very widespread phenomenon. Far from it! As already mentioned, the more prevailing trend is our omissions where we ought to speak up. Have you ever heard yourself use the following wording when referring to your conflicting staff: 'After all, they are grown-up people'? And have you heard yourself utter the words: 'My boss has the most awful way of conducting this meeting, and we never get down to a discussion of the actual cases. But I can't just give vent to my honest opinion at the senior staff meeting, can I...'? If so, you are not the only one!

In our capacity as business psychologists, we deal with many different assignments in many different organisations. We observe many leaders interact with their employees. We observe the coping – or non-coping – with problems. We observe discontent and grumbling employees spreading negativity rather than pulling their weight. They generate a negative atmosphere, setting poor standards of quality. Regrettably, such issues are far too seldomly coped with, in terms of leadership.

We observe leadership teams at completely disorganised meetings where people will be rolling their eyes and, subsequently, leaders will talk about frustrations, low energy levels, political wrangling, etc. But no one has the courage to take up the challenge.

To us, it has become evident that one of the major impediments is the considerable focus on well-being and involvement. This has generated a management taboo that leaves many leaders in a state of decision paralysis in which they dare not make any decisions, lead the way, pose challenges, or make demands, because they are afraid that this will result in poor satisfaction surveys, etc. Moreover, many leaders never really overcome their personal fear of being unpopular, of making mistakes, of speaking their honest mind, and of experiences. This leaves us with rudderless organisations that are practically void of direction and drive because of procrastination in respect of decision-making, hidden political agendas, and hypocrisy – circumstances that prevent the distinct charting of a clear common direction, cohesion in the performance of duties, and a shared commitment in respect of targets and key assignments. Such frameworks are in increasing demand in modern organisations of great complexity that are undergoing considerable changes.

The major reason why, in practice, leaders abstain from applying such learning, as they have received in courses and supplementary training, is the absence of maturity in organisations with respect to the interpretation of competence development as a strategic initiative rather than staff benefits. But the individual leader's lack of courage also plays a major role.

Emotional Courage – Fearless Leadership

With this book, we introduce the concepts of *fearless leadership* and *emotional courage*. We believe that fearless leadership and emotional courage may represent 'the missing link' in our perception of the reason why leaders do not 'just' act as they know they should and as theories prescribe as mandatory. Here, we found inspiration in a research article that focuses precisely on the significance of courage:

> There seems to be a theoretical gap between the need to act and the choice to act – between risk and moral action. This theoretical space can to a great extent be rationalised through the construct of courage.
>
> (Amos & Klimoski, 2014, p. 114)

Fearless leadership may refer to a number of actions. Basically, it is a matter of the ability to endure difficult situations, cope with discomfort, remain confident in circumstances of uncertainty, and to have the courage to stand out from the rest.

To be emotionally courageous, the leader must be able to hold aloof from others, yet continuing to be a part of a group. Further, leaders should be able to hold their ground in adverse or uncertain circumstances, even if this means enduring colleagues' anger – without taking a defensive position (Bregman, 2013).

Courage is not the absence of fear. Courage is to register the fear without submitting to it and be dominated by it, but rather to act in such a way as you experience as being necessary. Many of the leaders, with whom we have collaborated over the years, have found it really valuable and respectful to take themselves and their responsibility in their capacity as leaders seriously.

The replacement of conventional hierarchies and extremely well-defined roles and responsibilities by complexity and fluid organisations means an increased demand for leadership. It is necessary that, as the leader, you dare to lead the way, dare communicate your messages and visions, dare take responsibility, are willing to be persistent, are left unaffected by unpopularity, that you are willing to admit to own mistakes and to take responsibility for such mistakes. We consider it necessary that, in your capacity as leader, you are able and have the courage to:

- take initiatives to meetings and interviews that are important and necessary
- set goals and direction
- propose to settle disputes
- state your intentions clearly
- bring people around you together
- repair broken relations
- take responsibility and make decisions

instead of letting fear take over, resulting in you:

- pulling away from difficult situations
- seeking shared points of view
- helpfully making yourself available
- expressing yourself in general and guarded terms
- giving up easily

(Inspired by Holm, 2014, p. 70)

This book is about fearless leadership. About emotional courage in management. It is a tribute to all those leaders with whom we have worked – leaders who have courageously dared to put themselves into play, dared to train fearless leadership and generated such learning that constitutes the foundation for this book.

With this book, we hope to bridge the gap existing between leaders' knowledge of leadership and their failure to act on this knowledge.

Training is called for! You need to *do* something, as organisations are really in dire need of action. We therefore hope that the book will provide inspiration for courage and for getting started.

The book is intended as a practical guide for you who have a desire to get wiser on *yourself* as a leader and not on yet more management theory. The purpose of the book is to provide inspiration for new actions that will break away from established and inexpedient habits and behaviour, facilitating a more heroical approach to leadership. The book involves research and theory for the purpose of supporting and explaining focal points. We do, however, recommend that, in the course of your reading, you constantly focus on yourself and own learning. We have incorporated a set of questions for reflection in the reading process – questions that are intended to help you spot your own personal leadership as compared with the themes that are dealt with. Before rushing on, you should, in fact, try to pause for a moment's reflection on these questions.

The Heroic Leader

To a certain extent, the trend in leadership literature is to disavow a 'heroic' approach to leadership that focuses on which actions the leader in an organisation should take. The theory is that, for decades, there has been an excessive focus on the leader and a proportional lack of focus on the followers – the fans. The complexity that characterises today's organisations demonstrates the heroic leadership approach to be untenable. The overall social constructionist wave, by which, incidentally, we ourselves set great store, strongly pinpoints that the way the world and organisations are created is through language, in relations, and in interactions. Leadership is not feasible without followers. Occurrences and social worlds are understood in interconnected patterns. Leaders and employees will interact and collaborate on the creation of their realities.

We have no intentions of challenging the post-heroic leadership approach that encourages more distributed leadership understandings. We propose that leadership does not solely depend on one individual person or on one individual role. We do not hold the view that the leader – as a courageous hero – shall fight his way through obstacles and thus generate results. Our leadership work is decidedly focused on distributed leadership. We do experience, however, that social constructionist and distributed leadership approaches will, unintentionally, throw out the baby with the bath water, as it were – that the behaviour of leaders, their manner and leadership work in general, will in fact be of substantial significance. In management, we still consider it important to focus on the individual leader: Which of the leader's competences, emotions and behavioural patterns will play a significant role in the leader's importance to the organisation?

The complex, ambiguous, uncertain, and ever-changing world in which organisations are embedded is of importance in respect of which leadership model that will be feasible and practicable. Strategies – such as practised by the leaders of the American industry of the 1950s, during which era, leaders in charge of large corporate bodies were considered to be great heroes if they could lead as cost-efficiently as possible, whilst possessing the capacity for, singlehandedly, coming up with the master plan for the entire group – are no longer an option. Frequently, contemporary leaders will be employed by organisations in which the employees are more professionally knowledgeable than they are themselves. This means that no leader, on his or her own, will be able to comprehend or embrace all such matters as are required for the purpose of the implementation of a strategy. The leaders of today must therefore be capable of making themselves vulnerable: Know that they are imperfect, have the capacity for involving themselves in their environment, for demonstrating confidence, for asking for help, and revealing their doubts. Modern leaders are profoundly dependent on others – a circumstance which the leader must be capable of navigating. There is a need for leaders who still dare to be visionary, who know what they want, and yet dare to make themselves vulnerable, to be authentic and more human. It takes much courage and self-knowledge not to become liable to either the hard and lonely style or to the soft and vague style. At one and the same time, the leader of today must be able blaze the trail and take the lead as well as take a back seat and show trust. But, above all, leaders of today must possess considerable knowledge of self and be able to manage themselves as individuals in the leadership role in authentic ways which will, in fact, generate true followers. And, in this respect, virtues such as vulnerability, humility, and courage are crucial.

The Structure of the Book

In Chapter 1, we introduce the many leadership duties and situations which, in our experience, are factors that are particularly in play, or particularly in danger, in case of lack of fearless leadership. We discuss the importance that, as a leader, you get in touch with your visions and actually dare bring these into play. We discuss the importance that, as a leader, you must be able to act authentically in your leadership and, also, that it takes a good deal of courage to come forward. We discuss the significance of emotions in organisations of today and how important it is that, as a leader, you are capable of coping with emotions – also the complicated ones. We discuss the importance of conflicts – and costs – in organisations as well as the essential necessity that, as a leader, you do not hide behind the view that 'after all' your employees 'are grown-up people.'

In Chapter 2, we focus on such issues as may put obstacles in the path of your, the leader's, exercise of fearless leadership. We discuss leaders' discomfort at feeling unpopular, of being considered as providers, of the constant need of involvement, of hiding behind tools, of the pressure of work, or of the feeling that criticism is a no-go. We will touch upon how such matters originate in fear and how this fear will prevent leaders from acting as they should.

In Chapter 3, we will propose a few recommendations for how, as a leader, you may train your fearless leadership. One basic factor is that you will have to engage in and confront such situations as may make you fearful. Solely reading additional theory will be to no avail! We will, for instance, discuss how, through the application of action learning, you can set improvement goals and quite concretely bring these into play in you daily leadership in ways that will contribute to your development. We will also look into the ways in which your emotional intelligence can be trained and how, through mindfulness, you can cope with yourself and your fear in your everyday work.

Throughout the book, we use a number of cases for the purpose of illustrating our key points. These cases take their points of departure in the experience we have gained from all our meetings and projects with leaders and organisations in practice. Though fabrications in expression, these cases are based on a mix of actual organisations, situations, and persons.

Note

1 According to Foucault, genuine parrhesia solely occurs when originating from a less powerful position – addressing one that is more powerful. In instances involving risk taking, with much at stake. Albeit, owing to the much shorter power distance of the postmodern world, we deem it expedient to consider it in a wider sense.

References

Amos, B., & Klimoski, R. (2014). Courage: Making Teamwork Work Well. *Group & Organization Management, 39*(1), 110–128.

Argyris, C. (1990). *Overcoming Organizational Defenses. Facilitating Organizational Learning.* Boston, MA: Allyn and Bacon.

Bregman, P. (2013). *Why So Many Leadership Programs Ultimately Fail.* Harvard Buisness Review. https://hbr.org/2013/07/why-so-many-leadership-program

Buch-Hansen, E. (2011). *Her er din største frygt.* Lederweb, 11/18/2011: www.lederweb.dk/dig-selv/lederrollen/artikel/93385/her-er-din-storste-frygt-det-her-giver-dig-angst.

Foucault, M. (1999). *Discourse and Truth: The Problematization of Parrhesia.* Edited by J. Pearson. http://foucault.info/documents/parrhesia/index.html

Holm, I. (2014). *Det personlige lederskab.* København: Hans Reitzels Forlag.

Schutz, W. (2005). *The Human Element: Productivity, Self-Esteem, and the Bottom Line.* San Francisco, CA: Jossey-Bass.

Tamm, J., & Luyet, R. (2004). *Radical Collaboration: Five Essential Skills to Overcome Defensiveness and Build Successful Relationships.* New York, NY: HarperBusiness.

1 Why Fearless Leadership?

Over the years, we have worked with boosting the personal leadership performance of managers. And in the course of this work, we came to realise how large an extent of their management is affected by their personal leadership and, also, how important a role personal leadership will play. Their personal leadership will have an impact on their management in terms of operations, professional competence, human relations, and in terms of strategic management. This is because personal leadership will affect one's capacity for managing oneself, building relations, leading relations, establishing cultures, and much more. In the Figure 1.1, the American researcher and leadership consultant, Rob Kaiser, provides a very apt illustration of the need for the personal leadership or self-management.

We shall not discuss this model in detail but, as can be seen, all leadership is based on a person's capacity for self-management. To develop as a leader, you must be able to control yourself, your emotions, and your behaviour. This is hard, but fundamental, work.

We have come across many leaders who, in spite of strong project-management competences, considerable professional expertise and emphasis on human resource management and strategy, have experienced difficulties in coping with the practice of good leadership, because, one way or the other, they have gone wrong as humans. On the other hand, we have also met leaders with leadership responsibility for a staff whose professional capabilities are different from their own, who, in spite of not possessing any particular leadership tools, have yet been able to create very well-run departments because of high self-confidence levels and their capacity for adapting their leadership style to specific situations and people.

In 2014 (Petrie, 2014), Center for Creative Leadership (CCL) published a whitepaper in which a researcher had performed an extensive analysis of experts' assessment of the management of the future. A clear pattern emerged, namely that the experts were occupied by the question of how future management can be developed so as to cope

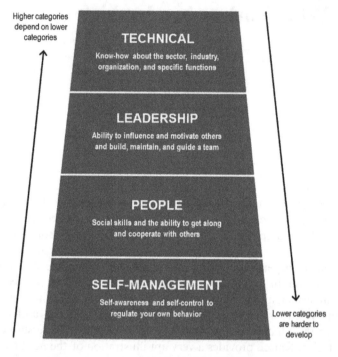

Figure 1.1 Managing yourself in a VUCA World. (Kaiser, 2017).

with the complexity and the pace of change that is symptomatic of the world and organisations of our times. In their interviews, they would speak of the need for putting a stop to the preoccupation with the development of management tools and the training of managers therein. It would, on the contrary, be more expedient to initiate the development of a more complex and adaptable mindset in managers. According to these experts, leaders have attained considerable knowledge about 'how' leadership should be construed, albeit failing to establish any competence in 'how to' conduct leadership. Leaders have excellent qualities when it comes to understanding and discussing what is implied by good leadership but, for their own part, they do not know how to cope with own continued development. In spite of having a profusion of knowledge and tools at their disposal, leaders fail to develop themselves, even though this is what, in fact, constitutes the actual and real requirement. Leaders must develop their own sense-making processes so as to encompass increased complexity. An example, taken from the whitepaper mentioned earlier, features a researcher's (Robert Kegan's) division into cognitive development stages. He distinguishes between three stages/steps of cognitive development in adults:

1 *The Socialised Mind*: Here, our surroundings' expectations from us, as well as their expectations in respect of good behaviour (and leadership), are crucial to our way of thinking and behaving
2 *Self-Authoring Mind*: Here, we have developed our own ideology, our own sets of values and an inner compass. We can make decisions and know how to set boundaries on the basis of this inner compass.
3 *The Self-Transforming Mind*: Here, we can take a step back and observe the limitations contained in our own ideology and values. We recognise the fact that they are but our own 'random' values – that there are others. We have become capable of coping with the multiplicity of meanings and have no need of polarisation, of dissociating ourselves from other opinions.

Leaders at the highest development stages are best equipped for coping with the complex and rapidly changing realities that are predominant in modern organisations. But only about 8 per cent of all leaders will actually reach the highest development stage. Hence experts argue that, in future leadership, it will be increasingly necessary to focus on the development of the individual leader's personal qualities. Today, we focus on leadership tools and competences. Frequently, when a leader finds it difficult to make decisions without clear instructions from his/her superior, this may be owing to the leader's fear of how his/her superior might react in the event of the leader's own decision-making rather than which decision-making tools should have been applied in the leader's decision-making process. When leaders are incapable of taking responsibility on their own and instead become too dependent on others, this may often reflect the fact that their fear of making mistakes, their fear of humiliation and disapproval, and their fear of feeling even more worthless constitute fears that have far too significant implications for leaders (Stein & Book, 2011). More so, than being an expression of the leader not recognising his/her responsibility.

Psychology has practically always been focused on the way in which fear generates a more one-sided understanding of one's surroundings. The activation of defence mechanisms may alleviate the fear. However, the reduced anxiety comes at a high cost by way of a reduced or distorted perception of reality. Thus, defence mechanisms may result in a person's wrong assignment of responsibility, reduce a person to stereotype traits, escapism from parts of reality, etc. (Visholm, 2004; Helth & Pjetursson, 2014). This is the direct opposite of what is needed according to the experts. We therefore consider the negotiation of fear to be an important factor to incorporate in the desire to develop a more complex and flexible awareness in leaders.

A variety of contexts and managerial functions require fearless leadership. In this chapter, we shall briefly outline a few of the most central elements in fearless leadership together with some of those arenas and areas of responsibilities that constitute important examples of situations in which fearless leadership is decisive.

The Double Job

The unpaid double job exists in all layers of society – not only in the business community but also within health and safety, teaching, politics, and public administration. Everywhere in the world people are concentrating their time and energy on hiding their limitations and uncertainties, trying to show up to their advantages, and to cover up their deficiencies (Kegan & Lahey, 2016, p. 1).

These days, we witness an immense waste of resources to take place in organisations. We use by far too much energy on impression management, comprising coming across as strong, hiding our mistakes, doubts, and uncertainties. Today, most organisations have experienced situations requiring retrenchment and the wielding of the cost-cutting axe. The initial move will typically target payroll costs and, next, the multitude of meal systems, flowers, coffee, etc. Only rarely, will the organisation address the circumstance that is typically the most cost-intensive, namely the double job. The spending of so many resources on coming across as competent, certain, clever, etc. is expensive in more senses than one. It is expensive in respect of quality; we contribute far from optimally when we use so many resources on impression management and self-protection. We do not learn from our mistakes and do not receive the help we need. This represents costs in respect of absence through sickness and stress. Double jobbing requires substantial human resources. Also, it means a significant increase in loneliness. Moreover, sickness among employees and leaders will also figure in the temporary-staffing accounts. And last, but not least, it will represent costs in the development area. A person's self-protection will lead to standstill. If one is to learn and develop, it is necessary to experience psychological confidence in oneself and to be able to reflect upon and share own shortcomings and uncertainties. In the swiftly shifting environment of today, the absence of personal development is a catastrophe for an organisation. The double job will contribute to minimise one's development as a person, which may be a severe source of employee burnout.

The Organisation as an Arena for Adult Learning

In former times, it was believed that the development of our brain would stop around the age of 20. A belief long since disproved by brain research. We, and our brains with us, develop throughout life. However, this development, and the way in which it takes place, will depend entirely on the types of learning and development environment in which we take part.

For many years, the motto: 'our employees are our most valuable resources' has resounded through the management literature and in the executive offices. This is rarely practised, however – except for the odd organisation offering free lunch, table tennis, a couch room, etc. But the employees 'are', in fact, the most valuable resource and, provided the true intensions of unleashing this, every employee should undergo continuing development, day in and day out. Not just specifically selected talents, but each and every staff member. If organisations succeed in this, real human potential will be unleashed, which will signify the creation of the very best prerequisites for the successful performance of duties, and, at the same time, people will thrive.

The organisations of the future consider the creation of healthy development and learning environments to be their most crucial strategy. Such environments will be characterised by psychological confidence in which no one will feel compelled to hide inadequacies, uncertainties, doubts, etc. – i.e. an environment in which the individual gets an opportunity to take on responsibilities that will be experienced as challenging, in the positive sense of the word.

Investing in human development as a long-term strategy takes courageous leadership. Especially considering all the critical issues that constantly pop up, requiring immediate attention. Likewise, it takes courage to insist on everybody undergoing development – also as persons. Not least considering the discourse that, in the order of things, insists that work is work, and hence focus should neither be directed towards personality nor towards the individual. Likewise, it takes courage for a leader to spearhead a scheme designed for working with own human traits and personality – and to be open about it.

To increasing extents, we are witnessing the performance of research that underlines the importance of development cultures in respect of the creation of innovation, creativity, and change. The research purposes and objects of scrutiny, for instance, comprise the importance of the development of mental complexity (see e.g. Kegan & Lahey, 2016), the importance of connectedness (see e.g. Chapman & Sisodia, 2015), and the importance of mindfulness, altruism, and compassion (see e.g. Hougaard, 2018).

Ask yourself:

1 Do you consider all human beings to be capable of undergoing development as a process running throughout life?
2 Do you, yourself, and your employees have concrete development targets that are public knowledge and with which you work on a daily basis?
3 Do you have a safe community against which you can lean, and which facilitates your courage to bring yourself into play?

Visionary Leadership

On the basis of research (Golemann et al., 2002) as well as experience, we know that, to the employees, visionary leaders will create commitment, a sense of community spirit and meaningfulness in the organisation and, further, that they are better equipped to retain talented employees. There is a wealth of theories occupied with the importance of visions. Most of these primarily focus on the significance of visions within and for an organisation, whereas others (e.g. Golemann et al., 2002; Goffee & Jones, 2006) also focus on the leader's role in this respect. The general consensus is, however, that visions play a considerable role in respect of uniting employees and generating energy, involvement, and direction.

Golemann et al. (2002) analysed a number of leadership styles. Their analyses demonstrated the visionary leadership style to be the most efficient. The background for this is, for instance, owing to the fact that visions will make the individual employee's work meaningful. You do not simply carry out a work assignment, you also contribute to a higher business goal. In practice, however, we very seldom experience leaders to be exercising this leadership style. Much too often, the leader will be completely wrapped up in operations without considering his/her visions relative to the core task for the organisation.

Asked about this, by far the majority of leaders will consider themselves to be inspirational and good role models. Actually, as many as 86 per cent (Hougaard, 2018). However, among employees asked the same question, i.e. how they experience their leaders, 82 per cent would answer that they experience their leaders as uninspiring (Hougaard, 2018). And measuring employee commitment, only 13 per cent of the world's employees will be committed, whereas 24 per cent will be decidedly uncommitted (Hougaard, 2018). Such figures provide food for thought. Not least because, according to Gallup's statistics, the concept of commitment constitutes the crux of the matter, signifying a major difference between committed and less committed workplaces: Relative to the most committed workplaces, their customers will be 10 per cent more satisfied, they will have 17 per cent higher productivity, and 21 per cent higher earning capacity. These workplaces have proportionally lower turnover of employees, non-attendance, and quality problems.[1]

Our lectures at the master's degree programmes in management are for instance based on research by Goffee and Jones (2006). One of the questions asked by Goffee and Jones is: "Why should anyone be led by you?" This question originates from their studies of successful leaders, and from what their studies propose followers to demand from their leaders. The point is that unless you, yourself, are explicit and conscious of your visions, targets, and values and are occupied with something that you are really enthusiastic about, it will be difficult to get anybody to follow you as a leader.

In the course of our work, we have often asked leaders what makes *them* so special, why others should follow *them* and what *their* personal visions and values mean to those they will be leading. The leaders found these to be difficult questions to answer. Some leaders will begin to tell us that they consider a good working climate in their department to be important. Only rarely will leaders promptly propose a fair idea of *their* particular qualities, and of *their* intentions. In their research and development processes with leaders, Goffee and Jones confirm this perception. We have spoken to leaders about the reason why, in spite of knowing how important this is, they are not exercising more visionary leadership. Answers and explanations are many and varied. One recurrent pattern, however, is that far too many leaders fail to consider themselves to be worthy leaders. At least not in respect of engaging in that part of leadership work that is about taking the lead and setting the course. 'Why me, in particular?' 'It was pure coincidence that made me a leader, but I've really got nothing to base it on,' 'I'm just not quite ready,' 'The time for it has not come yet,' 'Why should my perspectives be more important?'

Other leaders again, have completely lost track of their visions. Why did they become leaders? What, in their opinion, is important relative to their organisation's core task? What are they enthusiastic about relative to their customers? What can make them indignant? What are their dreams for their department or organisation relative to making a difference for their customers? Without visions, you are more or less reduced to a reluctant administrator.

Luis was the chief executive of a major NGO, an organisation with focus on the welfare of vulnerable children and families. Prior to his executive position, Luis had held a number of leadership positions – positions that he would eventually find a bit boring.

He lacked meaning in his work. After 100 days as the leader of the organisation, Luis had mapped out a string of circumstances at the head office which he considered to be profoundly inexpedient. However, he had become stuck in his situation, not knowing how to proceed. He grew increasingly frustrated but was incapable of action. His employees sensed Luis' annoyance but had no precise idea of what had gone wrong. Luis experienced a head office closing in upon itself, as it were – a head office having become inefficient and bureaucratic in its approach. As if the head office existed in its own right. A situation that left Luis extremely frustrated. He did not feel, however, that he would be in his right to call attention to this. He feared that his employees would become angry, worried, and react defensively.

For the first two years, he had been telling himself that he should sound out the situation and try to understand their position. But in the end, this was nothing but a poor excuse. When we met Luis, and he told us about his own background, about coming from humble circumstances, about fighting for the underprivileged, a change gradually came over him. Together, we looked into Luis' motivation for taking on the position and all the energies he had linked with the job. Luis had great aspirations to make a difference for vulnerable families. For large periods of his life, he had been a witness to the lives of families of deprived backgrounds – a fact that had made an impression on him. But because he had a relatively analytical and rational approach to many things, and pursuant to his upbringing, leadership-wise and academically, things should be rationally motivated. This approach had been quite consistent with Luis' need to feel competent and his fear of being humiliated if he was unable to explain matters. However, it was this very fear that had discouraged Luis from demonstrating his leadership qualities and disclose his visions, energies, and personal motivation in his job as a leader.

When Luis spotted these mechanisms, he initiated a number of contexts within which he could let his motivations, attitudes, and visions come into play. To his employees, this had a releasing effect. Initially, they had been virtually piqued by the feedback they received from Luis. But as Luis, at the same time, had the ability to communicate his visions and personal motivations, his leadership style resulted in a considerable rise in followers and an increased motivation at the head office, because his colleagues here perceived their roles and responsibilities for the organisation's business goal.

Try to pause for a moment's reflection upon visions within your own leadership style.

Ask yourself:

1 Where are my personal visions in my leadership work?
2 What am I enthusiastic about relative to the core task?
3 How, and how often, will I communicate these visions?
4 What prevents me from communicating my personal visions?

Overview

In continuation of visionary leadership, it is our experience that leaders are facing a tremendous task in providing overview. The world is changing at a more rapid pace than we are able to establish ourselves in new structures, habits, and routines; and, in many organisations, the work is of such a complexity that one may easily lose oneself in areas of expertise and critical problems. In our experience, a matter with which leaders are really struggling across all industries is lack of time and prioritisation. Employees and issues will perpetually be knocking at the door, and as leaders we will rush out the same door to solve such *ad hoc* issues. After all, it feels nice to be able to lend a helping hand. But the impact is striking; we completely lose our overview of direction, development, patterns in problems, culture, etc. If anything, the focus of contemporary leaders' contribution should be overview and direction. Where are we going? Why? How is teamwork around the organisation faring? How is our culture faring? What about budgets for next year, and how will this affect our current focus? But management meetings are characterised by short-term problems and grumbling about employees. Because leaders are, themselves, about to succumb to stress and pressure. We tear along, trying to rescue employees and customers, but we fail to reach out for the oxygen mask for ourselves. And this will have substantial and far-reaching impacts on the organisation. Fragmentations, recurrent problems, toxic work cultures, etc.

Peter was the managing director of his own business, which was based on the development of project-management tools for the private sector. He had founded his business three years before and had got off to a flying start. He had now reached a staff of 35, and the business continued to be flooded with assignments. Peter was an IT expert, and he loved working with IT development. He had, however, experienced an increasing frustration throughout the last year. More than 50 per cent of his working hours had been dedicated to issues concerning premises and administration and all sorts of practical problems. In increasing numbers, his employees were beginning to complain about various circumstances, and commitment was in free fall. This also applied to Peter. Each and every day, employees would be coming to his office complaining about everything, from issues with the copier to system malfunction pertaining to some of the IT systems provided for their clients. Peter would immediately leap to his feet and sort the various problems, but these would keep lining up in a perpetual queue. Having been wrapped up in everyday problems, Peter had become completely unfocused: exacerbated figures for client complaints. Dissatisfaction among his system architects. The culture pervading the business was characterised by a competitive mentality which was beginning to create toxic environments. The organisation of the employees had not been given any thoughts at all, and the absence of collaboration and knowledge-sharing was noticeable. Murmurs of dissent grew increasingly louder: 'chaos, lack of overview, where are we going,' etc. Peter had completely lost his overview as to how to define this new function that had arisen as a result of the pronounced growth of his business. He was still trapped in old habits relative to problem solving and had completely lost track of intended directions. He had lost focus as to the state of affairs concerning the general atmosphere among his staff members; and hence his business was in a state of total chaos.

Organisations are in dire need of leaders who dare to take a break and, on the one hand, communicate vision and direction and, on the other, open a dialogue with employees and take a reading of how the state of affairs is perceived, of opinion formation, and of what it will take to secure direction and a shared commitment. In fact, the provision of overview and direction is an important leadership function in business management, considering the eternal changeability, comprising political measures, that is sweeping across organisations of today.

The Monetary Standard of Emotions

We live in an emotional era. Emotions at workplaces have indeed come into focus. This also applies to the management literature (Tanggaard & Elmholdt, 2011). Emotions are no longer considered to be disturbing elements to be quashed. Now, they are rather considered asset resources that will constitute a major part of an organisation's life. Perhaps you have experienced a group among your staff in which conflict levels are high. And in this respect, you will have noticed how significant a part emotions play in employee collaboration or the lack thereof, in their perception of situations, in their prioritising, etc. Have you ever noticed the extent to which emotions will affect commitment – yours and that of others – at meetings pervaded by a negative atmosphere? And have you paid attention to the extent to which your own behaviour and way of coping – in your capacity as leader – will affect such crucial emotions?

At one of our courses, we asked a group of leaders the following question:

> Try to think back on your career. Try to think back on such leaders as you may have come across – leaders whom you admired and whom you considered to be effective leaders. On what was these leaders' effectiveness founded? Was it on their administration proficiencies? On their strategic capabilities? Because they were well-versed in management theory?

Not surprisingly, they answered that a leader's effectiveness was about having a strong personality, about being charismatic and strong on relations. And how does such strength work?

We are inspired by great leaders. Though we may try to ascribe their success to, for instance, strategy or vision, the truth is that great leaders work through the emotions (Golemann et al., 2002).

One of the most well-known researchers and authors within the concept of emotional intelligence, Daniel Golemann, claims to have proof that employees' emotional state of mind at the workplace accounts for close to 20–30 per cent of the financial results and, further, that between 50 and 70 per cent of employees' perception of the climate at their workplace can be ascribed to the actions of one person, namely the leader (Golemann et al., 2002).

Frequently, leaders affect cultures and atmospheres to a far higher extent than they are aware. When, with employees and leaders, we discuss their expectations of one another and of learning in respect of collaboration, many leaders are surprised to learn just how much weight employees will attach to precisely the leader's behaviour, frame of mind, and mood. According to Golemann, much of the emotional culture thus emanates from the leader. This is attributable to the fact that employees will typically pay much attention to their leader. Thus, many leaders have pronounced blind spots in respect of the impact their mood and behaviour will have on their employees. Research into feedback (Heen & Stone, 2014) suggests that precisely the 'blind spots' of leaders will signify 'hotspots' to others. In other words, such leader traits as are particularly noticed – traits that will have an impact on employees.

Hence, Golemann argues that the ability to steer collective emotions in a positive direction and clear the air of negative sentiments is a crucial responsibility, in the sense that it represents an underlying decisive factor which will affect all others. He applies the concept of emotional intelligence to describe precisely how vital it is for a leader to cope with own emotional reactions and relations. More specifically, emotional intelligence is about the ability to recognise and cope with own emotions as well as the ability to recognise other people's emotions and to cope with these relations. We shall return to this in Chapter 3.

Sam was the leader of the finance department of a major hospital. Having a background as a professional accountant, he had gone the leadership way because he liked to carry a great responsibility and have important duties. Over several years, Sam's department had undergone considerable change, comprising cost-cutting measures. He was well and truly fed up with his management and all the changes to which his department had been subjected. He told us how much time he invested in speaking with his employees, backing them up with respect to how infuriating he found the financial board's control system and all the wrong decision made by his superiors.

As Sam's leadership style was subjected to analysis, he realised how much his own behaviour would rub off on his employees. He had very much contributed to spread infection among his employees by way of negative emotions and dissatisfaction, whereas he had failed to keep an eye on the extents to which this leadership style had contributed with the reinforcement of negative attitudes and poor commitment throughout the department. In spite of his intentions to demonstrate loyalty and kindness towards his employees.

Sam opted for subjecting his leadership style and the underlying emotions to examination and reflection. He came to realise that, in many situations, he had been very much in disagreement with his superiors. He had, however, not been able to make his attitudes and opinions known, because he had not dared to challenge his superiors. He had thus built up an increasing sense of frustration and anger which, subsequently, he had neither been aware of nor been able to cope with.

Having searched his heart and preceding situations, Sam was able to spot his own reactions and actions as well as the adverse impact these had had on his employees. In the course of four months, Sam succeeded in changing his behaviour and leadership style. He began to exercise an increased upward leadership, proposing own perspectives in relation to the cost-saving process.

This way he took responsibility for contributing with upwards directed leadership within the system, thus enabling him to carry out loyal downward leadership in his own department. For the purpose of being able to lead with more consideration and a leadership style which would strike a more responsive chord in his own department, Sam simultaneously had to train his coping with own frustrations in ways and means that would not rub off on his department. To succeed, he in fact had to work with own frustrations in order that a new leadership style would find greater resonance and would not appear to be non-authentic. Therefore he, for instance, began to focus on such visions and opportunities as he himself perceived in the forward-looking changes and in the employees' contribution in this respect. Likewise, he shared his reflections with his employees, and thus took responsibility for his contribution in the preceding process. As a matter of fact, many of his employees had themselves experienced their leader's negative approach to be frustrating to a degree that had hampered their everyday work.

The American researcher, Brene Brown (2018), expressed the opinion that either you invest a reasonable amount of time and energy on employees' emotions, comprising their fears, or you will eventually have to invest an unreasonable amount of time in coping with inexpedient behaviour. When we are uncertain and fearful, fearing that we cannot allow ourselves to be vulnerable, we will be acting as humans on the basis of our defence mechanisms. And such behaviour may generate considerable inexpedient behaviour, e.g. our protection of ourselves, hiding our mistakes and uncertainties, saying no to assignments on the basis of rational arguments, we will constantly be taking a critical stance, etc.

It is important to address how, via one's behaviour, one may become a role model for one's employees and thus contribute to the creation of an organisation's culture. Gandhi is known for his statement: "Be the change that you wish to see in the world." If you want a recipe for how you change others, you must begin by changing yourself. We often meet leaders who have tried to change their organisations by introducing a change of organisational structures, procedures, organisation, etc. They will establish new teams, think out new strategies, issue new areas of responsibility to new leaders. In spite of this, it is often demonstrated that these leaders will not improve. It is not sufficient to have clear visions and strategies. If you, yourself, are emotionally disconnected from the organisation and your own leaders, both leaders and employees will behave counterproductively (Malandro, 2010). They will display silo mentalities, fight for resources for their departments, and go their own ways. We have worked with chief-executive teams that have carried out innumerable organisational adaptations without analysing how their own behaviour would contribute to a maintenance of problems. We have observed them participate in meetings and seen how they will continue to sit on the fence and keep their cards close to their chests, having no view at all as to how their own behaviour will affect others within the organisation. When leaders neither can, nor will, recognise these blind spots – how such inopportune behaviour will have an adverse effect on organisational results – it will be decidedly difficult to change the organisation.

Ask yourself:

1   Will I circumnavigate difficult emotions in myself or my employees, and what will be the consequences?
2   What do I fear will happen if I take more direct action relative to atmospheres and emotions at the workplace?

Authentic Leadership

When, today, emotions are so crucial, this is owing to the vital importance of the leader's dealing with himself as a person and with his own emotions. Emotions are infectious, and the leader's emotions even more so (Maddocks, 2017). This is to say that leaders really have to work with their emotional intelligence. A leader's fear or nervousness may be expensive in terms of much energy for employees who, consciously or unconsciously, will invest energy in stepping up their attention. In the event of any conflict in the management team and a leader's subsequent return from meetings emanating signals of anger or fear, such emotions will inevitably impact on the employees. Perhaps they will be more attentive in respect of unimportant matters because they will be on the alert, and hence become increasingly nervous. In case of conflicts in a department, and a leader who experiences this as unpleasant, the employees will be confirmed in their perception of conflicts as being dangerous and uncomfortable, unless the leader is open and informative about it.

From this point of view, a leader's capacity for acknowledging his emotions and coping with these is thus decisive for a workplace's capacity for investing energy in the core task. Similarly, the leader's social consciousness and ability to cope with relations are of major importance.

This is probably the reason why authenticity is one of the most popular buzzwords of contemporary management literature. And this for a good reason. Asked what they want most from their leaders, one of the most recurrent employee answers, across organisations, will be 'authenticity.' "We don't want leadership clones – noisy or quiet. We want real leaders" (Goffee & Jones, 2006, p. 7). All too often, we have talked with leaders about how difficult it is for them to be in contact with their emotions so as to, on the one hand, acknowledge these and, on the other, put them into play in relevant situations – rather than disguising them and, thus be controlled by them in all sorts of unconscious ways.

Leaders' biographies are quite popular today. You select a well-known and competent leader and write about how he or she goes about being so competent. Thus, a leadership recipe is uncovered which other leaders may follow to become just as efficient. Now, the exact result thereof is that leaders adhering to this strategy will not be authentic. There are no universal management characteristics. Management is situational (Goffee & Jones, 2006). Similar to the well-known Oscar Wilde quote: "Be yourself, everybody else is taken," you, the leader, should seek your answers to questions such as what you, yourself, have to offer. What are your particular attributes? And how would you put these into to play in management contexts in ways that will be relevant in a given situation or context? Many leaders believe that they should wear a professional mask at work. Having researched leaders' identities, Amanda Hay (2014) describes how leaders fail to perceive themselves as authentic:

> I can't believe I am saying this but as a manager of a big team, you have to put on this, it is almost like being an actor, isn't it to a certain extent? You play the audience, depending on who they are. I know this is against what I am supposed to be saying but I guess I always feel half the time, I am pretending, putting on a face that isn't the real me. Isn't what I talk about when I get home or what I do. And it is quite a relief to go "phew, I don't have to worry or think about anybody else."
>
> (Hay, 2014, p. 518)

Being authentic requires the courage to reveal and expose parts of oneself. That is to say, using oneself and one's practical judgement instead of hiding behind all sorts of theories and tools and thus risk standardised and manualised ways of coping that will not pave the way for authentic leadership. Authenticity is about being in contact with oneself, without making an effort. This means that you have a meaningful and cohesive narrative or story about yourself, your emotions, thoughts and behaviour with an equivalent continuity in your personal experience. You recognise yourself across the many leadership duties and situations within which you move, without losing yourself in the process. You can use your emotions in constructive ways and, on this background, cope with and grasp difficult situations.

As a leader you cannot evade situations of pressure. Pressure may result in unpleasant emotions of doubt, uncertainty, fear, and confusion. Such emotions may frequently be coped with and evaded by way of defence mechanisms which will help you to avoid these unpleasant emotions. But, as already mentioned, these defence mechanisms come at a cost. They prevent you from being in touch with 'realities' and inconveniences. Also, they may affect your behaviour in adverse ways, as they are out of touch with reality. Thus, the setting up of defence mechanisms may entail a behavioural pattern that will be either over- or under-involving. For instance, you may continue to involve your employees in a number of decisions and then proceed to plough the same furrow, even though what your employees are actually seeking are for you to make a decision. Or you may do everything on your own and fail to involve relevant employees in your decisions. Both behavioural styles stem from the fear of being ignored (Schutz, 2005).

On the whole, relevant and dynamic reaction under pressure will require that, as a leader and a human being, you will know how to let go of defence mechanisms and instead direct your attention towards how you, yourself, feel about it. You need to acknowledge your emotions. Next, it is a matter of converting such acknowledgement into behaviour that will be in compliance with your experiences. This is when authenticity occurs. And, as mentioned, this takes courage.

We have frequently come across leaders who will contain their anger or discomfort and try to appear composed when employees act in inexpedient ways. Other leaders will be profoundly annoyed with their peer leaders. They will attend management-team meetings, trying to count up to ten and pretend not to be absolutely exasperated by their colleague's long-winded and irrelevant monologues. They are easily seen through, though. There may, of course, be umpteen reasons why, in your capacity as leader, you feel inconvenienced by for instance coping with an employee whose behaviour will have a destructive effect. And you may easily become prone to reflect upon, or be annoyed by, the behaviour of this employee rather than reflect upon and cope with the reason why his/her behaviour will affect you the way it does. But it is no good to leave this feeling of discomfort untreated, as it were. It is necessary to convert it into a way of coping with the situation. Anger in leaders is a quite natural and legitimate emotion. It is a way of letting us know that our values, boundaries or ground rules have been infringed upon, that we feel under threat (Holm, 2014). Anger is data. It is not to say that, in order to be authentic, you should simply give vent to your emotions. Quite frequently, this will be counterproductive relative to what you want from the situation. What it does mean, however, is that you should remain in contact with such emotions and, on this background, come to a decision on what you want to do. This is the opposite of denial and avoidance of your emotional experiences, and it means that you should not take certain sides of yourself too seriously.

The following case is an illustration of a leader's non-authentic handling of experienced issues:

Brenda was a leader of ten years' experience. She was proud and of strong professional qualifications. She took an interest in her employees' work and emphasised quality. At one point, we got the opportunity to participate in the implementation of a new KPI (key performance indicators) concept in Brenda's organisation. We were not involved in this concept, as we were hired to coach the leaders in a leadership development programme. We had access to data by way of observing the leaders during KPI interviews with their employees.

As we knew Brenda from another assignment, she asked us to observe her. One of the things we noticed was that her behaviour would undergo significant change, all depending on which team a given employee would belong to. We subsequently discussed our observation with her, telling her that – in certain interviews – she would appear a bit strained, whereas in others she would be more relaxed. On this basis, Brenda told us that, against her will, they had 'inherited' a team and that, in her opinion, the members of this team did not assume responsibility. She considered them underperforming, and also, they generated a negative atmosphere. Asked why she did not share these experiences with the team, Brenda realised that she felt uncertain in the company of these employees, because she was afraid to give herself and her frustration away. Her way of coping with this uncertainty was to allow the team a much higher extent of autonomy than she, herself, found expedient. And she had managed to make herself believe that her reason for doing so was that, after all, it was an autonomous team which did not need her participation. In reality, her feeling of low self-esteem would prevent her from taking action. The result was, however, that her behaviour towards this team would demonstrate a low extent of authenticity.

Actually, the team had sensed that something seemed to be wrong, since Brenda would treat them differently as compared with her other teams. They had even asked her why she did not

attend their team meetings, to which she had just reacted with eva-
sive explanations. Obviously, they had also noticed that, in spite of
her explanations that she trusted them and considered them to be
autonomous, her behaviour towards them was distant and aloof.

Ask yourself:

1 How conscious am I in respect of my emotional reactions?
2 How often will I reflect upon my emotions and their background?
3 How often will I communicate these emotions?
4 How often will I put a lid on my emotions and yet be at the mercy
   of such emotions?
5 Where and when will I wrap my emotions too far away and, therefore, not react authentically?
6 How often will I reflect upon my leadership style and its effect
   within the organisation?
7 Do I know my own sets of values? Do I bring my values to work?
   How often will I communicate my values? And would my environment believe that I act in pursuance of my values?

Conflict Management

In 2008 OPP[2] published a report on conflicts at the workplace (OPP,
2008). Five thousand leaders and employees from nine countries were
interviewed about their attitudes to conflicts at their workplace. The
results were striking:

- 85 per cent experienced a need for coping with conflicts. On a
  weekly basis, the average employee would spend 2.1 hours on conflict handling. In England alone, this equals 370 million workdays
  that are annually lost on conflicts at the workplace.
- 27 per cent of the respondents had experienced conflicts leading to
  personal attacks, and 25 per cent had experienced this to result in
  sickness or absence.
- 67 per cent had consciously avoided physical contact with a
  colleague owing to a dispute at the workplace.
- 70 per cent found the capacity for conflict handling to be a 'very' or
  an 'extremely' important leadership quality.
- 43 per cent were otherwise of the opinion that their superiors did
  not handle conflicts as well as they should, whereas only 23 per cent
  of the leaders shared this point of view.

In Denmark and France, leaders had the most negative opinion of their competences in respect of conflict mediation.

Another study (Heen & Stone, 2014, p. 5) demonstrated that 63 per cent of senior-executive respondents considered the lack of courage and ability among their leaders in respect of having difficult interviews to constitute their most weighty challenge relative to efficient performance management. This survey did not measure whether the senior executives would then, themselves, take the difficult interview with their leaders. In our experience, however, this is regrettably far from being the case.

In far too many organisations, conflicts are allowed to go on for far too long. Much too frequently, leaders simply fail to intervene. 'After all, they are grown-up people' is the cliché constantly resorted to by leaders. In our experience, however, this statement is often a cover-up for lack of courage to intervene. The consequence will be poor decisions, poor structural separations, lack of collaboration, double purchase of equipment, absent synergies, lack of cohesion in solutions, customer/user confusion owing to conflicting signals, time lost from productive work – the list is interminable.

Conflicts require attentive leadership. The higher the conflict level, the more attentive the leadership needs to be. Quite often, the opposite is the case, though. The higher the conflict level, the more the leader seems apt to withdraw. We have discussed the matter of conflict management with many leaders. As will be dealt with in Chapter 2, one element that may, for instance, block the way for good conflict handling is the leaders' view that they are expected to be capable of controlling a situation. When employees will begin to talk over each other, to cry, or yell, a situation may be difficult to control. And, consequently, it will be difficult for a leader to feel whether he or she measures up.

We can for instance contribute with encouraging leaders to step into conflicts. Very often it is quite concretely a matter of leaders allowing themselves the opportunity to find energy and clear their schedule for preparing themselves mentally for stepping into the room, take possession of the room, frame the interview on conflict, put forward their perspectives and facilitate the meeting and subsequent meetings at which the conflict matter can be talked through. We frequently experience leaders who are well aware of what needs to be done. To do so, however, they need to summon up courage and energy to be able to cope with a concrete conflict. It is no good that you, as the leader, tries to smooth out the conflict, or that you are unable to control yourself in the process. Similarly, it is unfortunately seldom a good idea for a leader to take possession of a conflict-management tool with which the leader tries to handle the conflict. You just risk to become far too occupied with the management of the tool: 'Now, is where I say this or that, now I will act in this or that way.' This way you will lose yourself, your body as a sound box, as well as your practical knowledge and common sense relative to what to do in the situation. And, oddly enough, the situation will practically never develop as predicted by your tool.

Eric was the head of a medium-sized municipal school. He had ten years' teaching experience during which period he had, for instance, been a union representative and taken active part in many change processes and negotiations. He had intentionally applied for a managerial position at a different school, because he would not run the risk of getting into a tight spot in his new role as head of his former colleagues.

Eric was extremely pleased with his appointment as head of a school. At his age, this was something of a feat. At the school, he soon established good relations with many teachers and teacher teams, albeit with one exception, namely the team in charge of lower secondary education. At the first team meeting, Eric had witnessed a cheerless atmosphere, and tempers had flared – in particular when topics of conversation turned towards terms of appointment, working hours, and management. This surprised Eric, but he decided to stand his ground and to continue to attend team meetings according to plan. He would not act as the old heads of school, who had always shied away from cooperative problems.

When we met Eric, it had been three months since he had last participated in a team meeting for the lower secondary education. This actually caught him by surprise. But, lately, he had been quite busy, and he had convinced himself that there were more important things to be dealt with. At the last meetings Eric had attended, the team had been quite confrontational and demanding, just as the team members had been excessive in their complaints about the other teacher teams. The team had isolated itself and, in the staff room, the atmosphere had become increasingly gloomy. The collaborative interfaces, which were of such decisive importance to the interdisciplinary projects on which Eric placed so much emphasis, had foundered, and the teachers had again split up activities. Eric's visions of a cohesive school, in which educational standards would be actively applied for the purpose of generating inclusion and collaboration across teachers and educators and with open classrooms, were hanging by a thread.

As Eric realised this, he was – at one and the same time – surprised and embarrassed. How had he let it come to that? He pondered hard over this and understood that he had unconsciously avoided any contact with the lower secondary education team, and, likewise, he had disregarded the other teams' attention to the problem. Eric similarly realised that he was truly fearful of the teachers' anger and behaviour. He feared that they did not respect him and would criticise his leadership. At the end of the day, what he feared most was that he had neglected something; that, as to leadership, he was not on the right track; and that in direct contact with the teachers, he would be unable to handle himself. He could look back on a number of situations from which he had withdrawn and avoided important talks with the team. And he suddenly remembered how his stomach would cramp in these situations. It was on this background that Eric chose to take action. He was well aware that to do so, he would have to cope with his fear. He therefore prepared a number of concrete meetings with the team for which he had not only made a schedule but, to a larger extent, he had prepared himself mentally and emotionally. He expected fear to knock at his door. He accepted that it would be difficult. Nonetheless, he was determined to carry out his plan.

The meetings proved to be difficult. Eric chose to put his cards on the table and tell the team what he had noticed and how this did not tally with his approach to and desires for the school. This came as a major surprise to the teachers. Two of them became decidedly angry and blamed Eric for 'interfering with' their professional work. Eric had however prepared for this, and calmly stuck to his guns, claiming that this was his job as the leader. Later, the other team members would confess that, in a way, they were relieved. They, too, had experienced an adverse development and to be separated from good colleagues. In fact, they were very interested in collaborating on shared projects.

Eric used his experience from the meetings to outline the approach he intended to take when encountering conflicts and how he would cope with himself relative to matters triggered by conflicts.

Not many people enjoy situations of conflict. To a certain extent, most people tend to avoid them, if possible. We will frequently deceive ourselves, pretending that there are no conflicts or that they will solve themselves. This is very rarely the case. Sometimes, it is easier for us to become absorbed by employee reactions and the ways in which we believe them to be overreacting or otherwise behave foolishly. But as a leader you will have to acknowledge that what you fear in connection with a conflict is your own incompetence as to conflict management as well as the uncomfortable feelings you risk to experience. It is not conflict that you fear. It is your own reaction. Try to ponder this for a moment. The second you feel competent as a person relative to coping with conflict matters, you will no longer fear it. If you are willing to go through all such emotions, rather than avoid them, you will also – to a far higher extent – be capable of exercising such courage as will be required to cope with a situation which you do not know how to solve, a situation which you cannot control. Again, you will not become courageous without first experiencing vulnerability. In other words, have the courage to face the unpleasant emotions.

Ask yourself:

1   How often will I notice conflicts?
2   What will I tell myself, when I experience conflicts in my staff?
3   Think back to the last year: How was I affected by conflicts? Did I intervene?
4   What do I fear about conflicts?
5   What are my values, as a leader, relative to conflicts?

The Timid Leadership Team

Leadership teams also play an important part with respect to an organisation's culture, because the creation, influencing, or change of a culture is a complex and difficult leadership responsibility with which the leadership team will only succeed provided they act in concert. If, for instance, the leadership team wish to shape their organisation towards a culture characterised by a larger extent of self-management, they will only succeed provided they collaborate closely on this assignment. The point of departure for a healthy and efficient organisation is a leadership team with strong cohesion. A leadership team will issue a considerable number of decisions. Likewise, a leadership team will release significant energy to the organisation. If such energies and decisions are not cohesive and free from political intrigues and conflicts, the rest of the organisation will suffer.

The healthy organisational culture will thus begin by the leadership team. Only when a leadership team has the sufficient courage to work with its most basic and controlling emotions and suppositions, will it be possible for it to become a well-functioning and healthy leadership team. A healthy leadership team will save an excessive amount of energy. This is owing to the fact that members need not try to pretend that they are on top of things – which in actual fact they are not – and spend time hiding mistakes and uncertainties. Provided a healthy leadership team, both political intrigues and silo formation can be avoided. Such non-existence will release energy for organisational work focused on clarity, sincerity, courage, authenticity, and openness. In such cases, it will be feasible to create healthy departments in which employees will have the opportunity to generate results, avoid silo formation and animosity in respect of other departments and incomprehensible decisions.

When employees are led by a healthy leadership team, they can also be open about their mistakes, uncertainties, and doubts. This openness will support a healthy culture, facilitating development and flexibility and giving absolute priority to a good working climate. And this is where the management team shall take the lead. Nothing in an organisation will affect the learning culture more than the leadership team's capacity for receiving feedback and for being open and reflective. Leadership teams will, however, be put to the test by cultural challenges that are at least equal in size to the challenges facing the rest of the organisation. Indeed, much of an organisation's culture originates in precisely this unit. We have collaborated with many organisations that were troubled by job dissatisfaction, and many of those were also challenged by collaborative challenges in the leadership team. It is necessary that leadership teams develop courageous interaction to the benefit of the rest of their organisation.

Fortunately, both management literature and focus within the organisations are becoming increasingly directed towards the importance of the leadership team. To increasingly larger extents, the accepted trend is to organise and work in leadership teams. There are good reasons for this.

Never before were research on and general interest in leadership teams greater than now. Googling the concept *leadership team*, will generate close to 1,430,000,000,000 hits, and, likewise, the number of books published on leadership teams will grow steadily from one day to the next. The reason for this specific focus on leadership teams is, for instance, that:

- It is necessary for leaders to be established in a leadership team which constitutes their primary group. The alternative – that leaders feel that they rather belong downwards, in their department – will create fragmented organisations.
- In such complex processes as characterise many organisations of today, it is necessary to collaborate across. The alternative will be silo thinking and behaviour.
- Strategic thinking and strategic action should be exercised in parallel and be decentralised.

- The volume of information is increased and should be dealt with, better and faster, for the purpose of making sound decisions.
- Learning- and knowledge-sharing are strategically decisive concepts in organisations.
- There is a need for a shared leadership culture and enhanced focus on leadership.
- Research documents significant improvement potential in the role, function and effectiveness of leadership teams.
- Research demonstrates that, to a far greater extent, leaders feel better equipped for the solution of their departments' most important challenges, when they experience to be a part of an effective leadership team.

In spite of this knowledge, we constantly come across political intrigues, double jobbing, silo formation, and poor relations in our work as business psychologists. In our experience, this can be ascribed to timid interaction within leadership teams, with the basic dynamics being characterised by invulnerability, loneliness, and pretence. Such basic dynamics must be rooted out, if we intend to develop courageous communities and organisations.

A general perception of the development of leadership teams is that, in the course of time, a leadership team will automatically develop concurrently with its members getting to know one another. But actually, research (Trillingsgaard, 2010) has demonstrated that – to a far greater extent – development will originate when members of leadership teams dare to break habitual interaction patterns by approaching each other and by probing difficult issues. Research likewise demonstrates that development most frequently takes place intermittently rather than as a stable process over the passage of time. Certain aspects, that are particularly typical of leadership team development, are:

1 The personal style of each individual leader. The extent of the leader's reticence or dominance, how conflict-averse will he or she be? etc.
2 Team capabilities: How competent will the team be in respect of the facilitation of meetings, decision-making, application of visual aids, etc.
3 Relational depth: the degree of openness, direct style, conflicts, insistency, the sharing of emotions, etc.
4 Shared mental models: a shared understanding of purpose, duties, roles, visions, procedures, etc.

The challenge is that developmental leaps will, among other things, depend on a member who will speak bluntly. Thus, the concept of leadership meetings constitutes a most annoying element to leaders, in particular comprising unclear targets and agendas together with process derailment in respect of agendas (see e.g. Bang & Nesset Midelfart, 2012; Bang et al., 2015). No one will speak up, however. Rather than speaking bluntly, most leaders opt for the safest solution and bite their tongue. At our leader coaching courses, we frequently meet leaders who are frustrated by their leadership meetings. And we often witness meetings of leadership teams at which participants will remain sitting at the fence, and at which complicated matters representing opposite interests will be skated over. The result is that leaders will neither coordinate their work nor pull in the same direction. They fail to commit in compliance with the shared business goal.

Hector was a university dean. When he took over the appointment, four smaller institutes had merged, and cohesive results were important. Hector considered this to be quite a tall order; and he was frustrated that the schools continued to refer to 'them' and 'us' – complaining about who did the most work, etc.

We attended a management-committee meeting at which Hector announced the introduction of yet a shared administrative operating system. He communicated this with firm conviction, thus silencing practically every other committee member. They had experienced Hector to be stubborn, and that it was practically impossible to make him change his mind once he had made a decision. They knew from experience that he would react with annoyance, should anyone go against him, because he was firm in the belief that he was always right. One dean sat quietly, musing on the talk he had had with his heads of department a few days earlier. Here, they had had a long debate on the issue of the many administrative systems. Hence the dean dared to voice an objection.

Hector rose and walked about in the room. He began to defend and explain the administrative system. The dean then held his tongue. Prior to the meeting, we had talked with Hector who was profoundly frustrated because the employees failed to use the administrative systems as they were supposed to. Also, his deans failed to put pressure on their heads of department in order that they would force through the use of the systems. Hector was not at all aware how his own unapproachable manners would cause the deans to clam up and, consequently, desist from linking up with initiatives.

When, subsequently, we interviewed the deans about how they had experienced the leadership meeting, they would practically all state that they feared Hector's angry outbursts. Several had tried to express their disagreements in various circumstances, but they had experienced how Hector would resentfully brush aside their objections. Over time, they had practically grown accustomed to shut up and then go back and do precisely what they, themselves, considered the best approach. Quite frequently, completely contrary to Hector's and other deans' points of view.

Afterwards, we had a lengthy chat with Hector. He was furious and frustrated with the incompetence of his deans. Deep down, however, he was really scared that he was not equal to the task and that, in two years' time, he would be dismissed – and the object of ridicule. He feared that, after all, he did not possess the competences required. And, at meetings, he was truly afraid of losing face.

We discussed the meeting and his behaviour with him, and we talked about how it was precisely this behaviour that would create what he in fact was definitely averse to. He was amazed to see things in this perspective. He was convinced that he was much more behind the scenes and that his behaviour was nothing but a response to the deans' lack of active contribution. He realised how his own fear of failure had made him act in ways which were, in fact, on their way to become a self-fulfilling prophecy since, in no circumstance, would he be able to succeed with his project without the backup and commitment of his deans.

Consequently, Hector opened the next meeting by disclosing his changed perception. He made visible his earlier blind spots and asked for feedback. The deans sat gaping. There was a pause. There was hesitation. What was this? The deans were not easily convinced of the good intensions. But eventually they were won over. And then, the leadership team got to work! By changing himself and his behaviour, Hector succeeded in preparing the ground for dialogues on interaction and shared responsibility. These dialogues emphasised that difficult issues should be dealt with in depth and, further, that disagreements and differences were cultivated in order that the work of the deans would reveal commitment and coordination. In the course of eight months, the leadership team succeeded in establishing three major projects of interdisciplinary natures in which the deans were committed to the shared objectives, pulling in the same direction. To them, this was a completely novel and trail-blazing way of working.

The correlation between courageous leadership teams and courageous leadership is close. Where, as a leader, you experience that you are expected to appear as invulnerable – not knowing whether your leadership colleagues will back you up – the capacity for courageous leadership, for being visionary, entering into conflicts, being persistent, being vulnerable, etc. will be much more reduced than if, together within the leadership team, you dare to be vulnerable, challenging, and supportive. Because to the fearless leader, it makes a world of difference to be a part of a fearless leadership team.

Ask yourself:

1 Dare I be vulnerable in my leadership team?
2 Dare I speak my mind, give, and seek feedback from my own leadership team?
3 How do we cope with disagreements and conflicts in our leadership team?
4 Do we share commitment in respect of difficult decisions, or will members do what they consider to be the best solution?
5 Do we interfere with each other's work areas, or will we leave one another to proceed according to low standards?
6 Are we capable of creating cohesive solutions and of coping with interdisciplinary problems and projects, or do we mainly work according to the silo mentality?

Notes

1 www.slideshare.net/adrianboucek/state-of-the-global-workplace-gallup-report-2017
2 OPP is a European distributor of numerous test tools. www.opp.com/en.

References

Bang, H., & Neset Midelfart, T. (2012). *Effektive Ledergrupper.* Olso: Gyldendal

Bang, H., Neset Midelfart, T., Molly-Søholm, T., & Elmholdt, C. (2015). *Effektive ledergrupper – For bedre udvikling, implementering og tværgående sammenhæng.* København: Dansk Psykologisk Forlag.

Brown, B. (2018). *Dare to Lead: Brave Work, Tough Conversations, Whole Hearts.* New York: Random House.

Chapman, B., & Sisodia, R. (2015). *Everybody Matters: The Extraordinary Power of Caring for Your People Like Family.* UK: Penguin.

Goffee, R., & Jones, G. (2006). *Why Should Anyone Be Led by You? What It Takes To Be An Authentic Leader.* Boston, MA: Harvard Business School.

Golemann, D., et al. (2002). *Primal Leadership: Realizing the Power of Emotional Intelligence.* Harvard Business Review.

Hay, A. (2014). 'I Don't Know What I am Doing!': Surfacing Struggles of Managerial Identity Work. *Management Learning, 45*(5), 509–524.

Heen, P., & Stone, D. (2014). *Thanks For the Feedback: The Science and Art of Receiving Feedback Well.* New York, NY: Viking/The Penguin Group.

Helth, P., & Pjetursson, L. (2014). *Ind i Ledelse. Lederens arbejde med sig selv og sin læring.* København: Akademisk forlag business.

Holm, I. (2014). *Det personlige lederskab.* København: Hans Reitzels Forlag.

Hougaard, R. (2018). *The Mind of the Leader: How to Lead Yourself, Your People, and Your Organization for Extraordinary Results.* Boston, MA: Harvard Business Review.

Kaiser, R. (2017). *Managing Yourself in a VUCA World.* LinkedIn article: www. linkedin.com/pulse/managing-yourself-vuca-world-rob-kaiser/

Kegan, R., & Lahey, L. L. (2016). *An Everyone Culture: Becoming a Deliberately Developmental Organization.* Boston, MA: Harvard Business Review.

Maddocks, J. (2017). Does the Emotional Intelligence of Leaders Influence the Emotional Climate of the Organisation? *Assessment & Development Matters, 9*(3), 10–15. www.jcaglobal.com/leaders-emotional-climate.pdf

Malandro, L. (2010). *Fearless Leadership. How to Overcome Behavioral Blind Spots and Transform Your Organization.* New York, NY: McGraw-Hill.

OPP. (2008). Fight, flight or face it? A global research report by OPP® in association with the Chartered Institute of Personnel and Development, July 2008.

Petrie, N. (2014). *Future Trends in Leadership Development.* CCL. http://insights. ccl.org/wp-content/uploads/2015/04/futureTrends.pdf

Schutz, W. (2005). *The Human Element: Productivity, Self-Esteem, and the Bottom Line.* San Francisco, CA: Jossey-Bass.

Stein, S., & Book, H. (2011). *The EQ Edge. Emotional Intelligence and Your Success* (3rd edition). John Wiley and Sons.

Tanggaard, L., & Elmholdt, C. (2011). Autentisk ledelse i den emotionelle organisation. In L. Tanggaard & C. Elmholdt (eds.). *Følelser i ledelse.* Århus: Klim.

Trillingsgaard, A. (2010). *Udviklingsepisoder i ledelsesteams.* Erhvervsph.d.-afhandling ved Center for Dialog og Organisation, AAU. Århus: Udviklingskonsulenterne A/S.

Visholm, S. (2004). Organisationspsykologi og psykodynamisk systemteori. In T. Heinskou & S. Visholm (eds.). *Psykodynamisk organisationspsykologi – på arbejde under overfladen.* København: Hans Reitzels Forlag.

2   What Blocks the Way?

In this chapter, we will discuss some of the pitfalls that contribute to the creation of fearful leadership. They all share the fact that we are much too unwilling to experience disagreeable emotions. We are a pain-avoiding society in which we unconsciously take it for granted that disagreeable emotions are to be avoided. We prefer to avoid conflicts, pain, loss, rejection, criticism, uncertainty, etc. Upon careful reflection, we realise this to be the goal of dead people. After all, we cannot go through life without discomfort, just as we cannot be competent leaders unless we dare to face the unpleasant situations that are invariably linked with being a leader.

At the end of the day, it is quite often a matter of low self-esteem. More leaders than would be supposed are struggling with low self-esteem. A fact that, on a daily basis, hampers them in their leadership. This prevents them from coming to the fore, make decisions, stand their ground and take responsibility. When persons have low self-esteem, their leadership tools will not be brought into play in a positive way. Very often, it is not until a leader dares to put aside all the tools and emerge as a person, that the leader becomes effective in his leadership. This is the moment when the leader is authentic and rings true. At this stage, the leader can act courageously. However, courage may fail which, for instance, occurs in connection with low self-esteem.

Lack of courage is practically synonymous with lack of self-confidence. A person without self-confidence is generally not apt to act courageously – to take risks. In short, the greater a person's confidence in him- or herself, the greater his or her tendency to act courageously (Amos & Klimoski, 2014, p. 116).

Surprisingly many leaders recognise having a low sense of self. We ask ourselves and them whether this is something they otherwise recognise in their lives, or whether it is something that has developed gradually. Naturally, the answers are somewhat varied. Some leaders recognise having lacked a positive sense of self, right from their earliest years. They relate about childhoods in which parents were unable to provide safe attachment and backup. Childhoods in which they did not really feel well-liked or important. Others will relate about unfortunate jobs in which they have experienced poor collaboration with peer leaders or employees.

Also, the impact of low self-esteem transpires in different ways. Some leaders will stow away their low self-esteem, pretending to be more self-confident than they actually feel. They step onto the stage, take the floor, and force through their opinion, but they fail to listen. In some cases, they will be over-controlling and too interfering, thus exercising micromanagement. They fail to include others – also in cases when this is the obvious strategy. As persons, they are aloof, and once in a while (e.g. during holidays) they will suddenly experience the gnawing feeling that, in actual fact, they do not feel well liked, and this matters much more to them than they let on. Other leaders will creep along the walls. They struggle to solve concrete and occupational tasks. They do not take on leadership and avoid conflicts. They will involve others – also unnecessarily. They open up too much, becoming too familiar. To them, the feeling of poor self-esteem typically fills up more in their daily lives. There will be good days, but on many days, they will leave work with a bad gut feeling. Did they actually do the right thing? Would their superior consider them competent? And what did their employees think?

According to Schutz (2005), the secret is to be flexible in one's behaviour: It is necessary to be inclusive, controlling and open to extents that are adequate relative to the situation. Basically, the background for this is rooted in self-esteem, says Schutz. It is our self-esteem that lays the foundation for our behavioural flexibility and for how often or seldom we are controlled by our fear. People with high self-esteem are more self-contained and will thus not have the same propensity to try to avoid disagreeable situations. They will not be as afraid of being ignored, humiliated, or rejected. Or they consider themselves capable of coping with emotions. In the next chapter, we will look into the development of a more courageous leadership style based on self-esteem.

The list below is a selection of some of the areas that are most frequently mentioned as issues with which leaders are struggling:

- You do not like to be unpopular
- You believe you must practice involvement
- You consider yourself a provider
- You believe that criticism should be banned
- You do not care for asymmetry
- You believe that you must be confident
- You shy away from decision-making
- You believe a heavy workload to be a redeeming factor

- You believe that you can hide behind tools
- You consider vulnerability a weakness

You Do Not Like to Be Unpopular

You may recognise these situations:

- Scenario 1: You have a competent employee whom you appreciate. The annual KPI interview is approaching. You are aware that this employee has set his/her sights on participation in an expensive course programme, which you cannot afford. But it is darned hard to bring yourself to say so.
- Scenario 2: Your employees have been used to follow a very flexible work schedule – to come and go at their own convenience. Owing to new assignments, you consider enhanced collaboration across to be a necessity, and this will require increased attendance. But you are not keen on making such a demand.

Can or shall a leader be constantly popular? 'No – of course not' is the typical reply by most respondents. But, in practice, we repeatedly experience how not striving to be popular is actually much more difficult than assumed by the leader.

At one point, we worked with the head of a university department. This leader, who had himself been attached to the department in a research position, had accepted the managerial position because his colleagues had proposed him as the natural successor to the former head of department. While a colleague, the present head had enjoyed considerable support from his peers, partly because he was a professional capacity, but as much because he had involved himself in various committees for the purpose of securing satisfactory employee influence.

Not long after his appointment, the faculty launched a major strategic process where one of the objectives was to establish enhanced strategic focus and cohesion. In practice, one of the decisions was that the research leaders should take more responsibility and work more strategically. Strictly speaking, the new head of department was in agreement. But communicating this decision to the research leaders proved to be more difficult than he had expected. He was actually fearful of the research leaders' reaction. Would they be annoyed? Would they consider him a turncoat? Would they shy away from taking responsibility? Would they refuse? And what then? For months, the leader struggled with emotions that inhibited him from taking action. He discovered a considerable fear in himself – a fear that prevented him from taking the necessary organisational decision.

Through fundamental reflections, he discovered that, among other things, this fear was ascribable to the fact that he did not want to be unpopular. In fact, he feared his employees' reaction to a degree that left him paralysed. Though having all the right arguments, he was convinced that the research leaders would take a different view and be annoyed with him. These reflections enabled the head of department to hold his fear a bit at arm's length and reflect upon how he was affected by this fear and how to act without letting fear become a dominant influence. He succeeded in having difficult but good talks with the research leaders about the strategy of the institute, his role as a leader in this, and what was required by them in their capacity as research leaders.

One research leader chose to give notice, but the other research leaders chose to involve themselves in the strategy and work actively towards the creation of research projects that would underpin the strategy, whereas deselecting projects that would not.

As mentioned in the introduction, we all have a basic need to enjoy popularity and an equivalent fear of rejection. This will affect our behaviour relative to our openness and confidentiality in our dealings with other people. If a leader is decidedly fearful of rejection, this may impact adversely on his/her leadership to an extent that will prevent the leader from making such decisions as are deemed necessary, because of the fear that employees or colleagues will cold-shoulder the leader's proposals. Perhaps the leader is on too good terms with his/her staff in order to keep them close and thus attempt to secure good relations – to feel likeable. Or perhaps the leader will dissociate him-/herself from staff members, appearing callous and stand-offish for the purpose of avoiding rejection.

Ask yourself:

1 When was the last time I was unpopular?
2 Why?
3 How was my personal experience of this, and what did I do?
4 Do I recognise the fear of being unpopular?
5 How do I feel about being persistent, even though this upsets my staff or makes them resentful?

6 Are there any existing situations with which I have failed to deal for fear of becoming unpopular?

7 What would I do if I were free of this fear?

8 How would this comply with my values as a leader?

You Believe You Must Practice Involvement

You may recognise this situation:

- Scenario: You attend a staff meeting. Actually, your assessment of the situation is that a new approach to the planning of work assignments will be absolutely essential, and also far more powerful. However, you feel that you will have to involve your employees. You half-heartedly open the round by asking their opinion. You feel you ought to. The problem is, however, that – regardless of their reaction – you consider the introduction of new ways of organising things to be essential.

The democracy discourse at workplaces is flourishing. For years, leaders have been assailed with courses and narratives pivoting on involvement, inclusion, ownership, listening, etc. And, at workplaces, attitudes as to how things should be done are many and varied. We frequently experience how change processes, new initiatives, new organisations, and so on have become deadlocked. And, not seldomly, we witness leaders who have invested considerable time and energy in the preparation of inclusion processes in which employees should be heard and taken into consideration. The occurrence of many, and frequent, conflicting interests and ideas will engender problems.

To whom should the leader listen the most? How to take everybody's interests into consideration? Etc.

At one time, we were invited to a larger educational institution for the purpose of facilitating the introduction of team structure. As always, we began by asking detailed questions about the background for this desire. What was team structure intended to support within the organisation?

Unlike other organisations that simply want to introduce teams just because this is in vogue, this particular leader actually had a number of valid reasons as the nature of tasks and a changed organisation had prepared the ground for team structure. We inquired about the process status. What had already been done, and for what did they need our assistance. The leader explained that, two years earlier, he had already proposed the idea and that, since then, he had held several staff meetings about the idea. Responses to his idea were mixed. The majority found it a tremendous idea, whereas a few took a more critical position. The leader's words to us were: "I so much want to involve everyone. I really wouldn't want to ram it down their throats. After all, it's their work, and they know best." The leader's reluctance to force something on someone, together with the notion of employees who know best, may be typical examples of the involvement discourse having become too entrenched. In this example, the leader was of the preconceived opinion that he would be guilty of poor leadership, if he simply made the decision. After all, he did not want to play the part of "J.R. from Dallas." He felt that he should involve and coach his employees in such solutions as might be preferable. But the consequence may be disadvantageous.

In this case, the consequence of the leader's hesitance was his department's failure to adapt to the organisation's demand. The employees had not, to adequate extents, been able to cover for one another; and, likewise, they had failed to share knowledge to required extents. New colleagues were not sufficiently instructed, assignments fell between two stools, etc. When we discussed the situation with the employees, they did in fact voice the opinion that they wished the leader would 'back off.' They were truly fed up with the repeated discussions of this topic. They had reached the point where they simply wished to move on.

Many leaders feel trapped by express demands for involvement and democracy. In our talks, we usually apply the metaphor of leaders being entrapped in a discursive prison, in which predominant discourses will disqualify or even taboo the power-asymmetric aspect in management. Leaders find themselves chasing a consensus that cannot possibly be reached. In the words of the philosopher, Ole Fogh Kirkeby, "Where there is consensus, there is lying" (Kirkeby, 1998, authors' translation).

To many leaders, the great leadership movement about the engaging and including leader has caused much confusion, frustration, and – not least – decision paralysis. Leaders want to listen, motivate, and involve, and they are at sixes and sevens whenever they get the urge to make a decision. Leaders fear that they will not measure up to the right leadership style. They fear employee criticism – to be accused of being dictatorial and not listening. They fear the annual job satisfaction survey in which their superior will want to know the reason for the red figures for column 14 about involvement, or column 20 about winning applause.

The effect of predominant leadership discourses is that some leaders have become far too good at listening to their employees. They have, to far too great extents, begun to let their employees lead. This means that, fundamentally, employees will be setting the course and take the lead, which leaves a fragmented and uncoordinated organisation, lacking cohesion. In our view, there is considerable demand for, and accountability with respect to, the creation of direction, cohesion and a shared commitment relative to the organisation's core task and strategies. This will require leaders who are not overly intent on listening to their employees – in ways that will entail fragmented organisations. At the same time, we acknowledge that, precisely because of the pronounced foothold obtained by the democracy discourse in many organisations, it is often important that, in your capacity as leader, you know how to listen to and understand your employees' perspectives. Frequently, the employees actually do possess important knowledge that may be central to incorporate in the qualification of a process or decision. However, the leader must meet an important objective, namely the securing of commitment relative to a shared direction, which is also about ensuring that no individual's separate goals or demands are given the inside track and thus come to take the lead. The leaders are the ones who set the overall course, without fail, thus providing employees with the opportunity to lead themselves and take responsibility so as to be qualifying for the organisation and the shared task – rather than accommodate their own small corner of a core task.

The considerable focus on involvement has generated a management taboo that leaves many leaders in a state of fear – fear of taking the lead, of making decisions, and of getting straight to the point. In short, to be frank and to lead. Which is why, to very high extents, they abstain from doing so. Not only will many circumstances suggest that involvement does not always have the desired effect, as the increased degree of involvement also leaves leaders with reduced resolve. Leaders are left with the feeling of losing their footing in matters of decision- and demand-making, which will engender a state of inertia that will have a protracting impact on necessary change processes.

Steen Visholm very aptly states that:

> If, using our common sense, we can acknowledge that authority relations are necessary in a complex society in which everyone depends on everyone – albeit in different ways, we must also acknowledge that autonomy shall be construed as the right to negotiate and express one's opinion, not to call the tune.
>
> (Visholm, 2004, pp. 90–91, authors' translation)

As mentioned in the introduction, all humans have a need to feel important. This, combined with the fear of being ignored, will affect a person's behaviour relative to the degree of mutual contact we seek to establish. Leaders with a pronounced need to feel important, or with tremendous fear of being ignored, may be at risk of causing excessive involvement; of asking the opinion of others far too frequently; of constantly seeking out others – and their opinions. And hence they lose their propensity for independence – for taking responsibility.

Obviously, you – the leader – must be able to involve, to listen. But you must also be capable of assessing what the task requires, rather than letting your own psychological needs be the determining factor for whether to practice involvement or not. Indeed, we also know leaders who will involve far too seldomly, a fact that may stem from similar psychological mechanisms, e.g. a fear of not coming across as strong. It may also be rooted in arrogance. This is, in every way, highly inexpedient but, also, a different kettle of fish altogether.

Ask yourself:

1   Am I over-involving my employees?
2   What might I fear by refraining from involvement?
3   To what do I make myself believe that involvement should be a means?
4   How do I feel about single-handedly making a decision, knowing that this will not be popular with everyone?

You Consider Yourself a Provider

You may recognise these situations:

- Scenario 1: The annual job satisfaction survey has just been published. You will have to discuss the survey with your employees. There are a few red fields, and you hear murmurs of dissent to the effect that it really is a disaster that the employees are not given the time necessary for the performance of their assignments. A negative atmosphere arises in the course of the meetings with the employees: 'It's high time the management took action. Did something.' You are left with the feeling that it all depends on you, albeit the problem is of such a complex and cultural extent that you cannot provide a solution on your own.
- Scenario 2: You have recently been appointed to your leadership position. You have learned from the employees that your predecessor seldom contributed to problem solving. Also, you have observed that there have been prolonged difficulties in the department. You decide that, now, you really have to do something about

this. It is your responsibility as a leader. You will have to sort out these matters.

Anna was the leader of a hospital HR department. Because she liked to work with people and their job satisfaction, she had always had a desire to become a leader. She had already experienced a lot in her career, and – as a consultant – she had been quite involved in leadership. In her role as consultant, she had always stressed that job satisfaction and working environment constitute decisive factors in the functioning of an organisation. She had therefore made provisions to ensure the hospital's performance of the tri-annual job satisfaction survey. Fortunately, she had good contacts within the world of consultancy, and she therefore succeeded in securing a good agreement on a survey.

She was really excited when she received the result concerning her own department. In fact, she looked forward to reading it. She had already accomplished much in her department and had made performance and development interviews with all employees. She had been extremely listening and shown an interest in everyone. Reading the conclusion was a tremendous disappointment to her. The result was only average! Though on the point of having a fit, she fortunately remembered her good tools, and hence chose the curiosity approach – according to which she would ask detailed questions about the reason for the responses. She organised dialogue meetings during which the employees were encouraged to word their experiences and clarify what she could improve to achieve enhanced levels of job satisfaction within the department. Ideas were voiced in abundance – and many of these indicated that the employees wanted improved working conditions, greater appreciation with respect to their work within the organisation (in particular from the physicians' team), and better offices. Working in those three-desk offices were virtually impossible! They more-over experienced their meetings to be malfunctioning.

Though a bit overwhelmed by all these issues, Anna got to work. She organised meetings with the hospital management about offices, meetings with the physicians about their approach to her employees, and she practiced being more appreciative towards her employees. As a concrete initiative, she also tried to change the meeting structure as well as her chairing of the meetings. At meetings, she became more involving, applied new methods for shared dialogue, etc. Nonetheless, she just experienced a staff that continued to demonstrate minimal commitment at meetings. The employees appeared disinterested, as if they just wanted to mind their own business and own tasks and considered meetings to be a waste of time.

Like so many others, Anna was facing a hopeless task. She had become a provider. A provider of a good working climate.

There is a widespread tendency for organisations' cultures to position leaders as providers. There are anonymous workplace assessments to be read and interpreted by leaders, and according to which leaders shall make action plans. All the action required from employees is their ticking off of boxes. But when all is said and done, they have stated where the shoe pinches, haven't they? And next, they expect the management to do something. And many leaders swallow the bait and bring themselves in position as the provider of good working climates: What can I do in order to provide an improved working climate for you? But the thing is that, without increased shared responsibility, it will only very rarely be possible for one person, even though this person is a leader, to singlehandedly change the working climate of a department. Employees should openly declare any dissatisfaction, rather than hide behind the anonymous workplace assessment. And leaders must persist in holding everyone responsible for the creation of the working environment surrounding us.

Research (see e.g. Kristensen, 2008) within this field suggests that, to a far greater extent than earlier, working environments reflect relations at workplaces, beyond very permanent structural relations that can be changed. But the predominant 'them-and-us' and 'a-and-b teams' approach existing within many organisations suggests an adverse solution, according to which the responsibility for good working climates and environments is unilaterally placed with the management. Indeed, there are also examples of the opposite – of leaders disclaiming liability, allocating all responsibility to autonomous teams – 'You are, after all, professionals and should be capable of coping with collaboration and working climates within the teams.' But, in an overall perspective, organisations are often culturally affected by leaders being positioned as providers and by their own, subconscious, positioning of themselves as providers. We believe that leaders need to insist on a shared responsibility if a successful development of e.g. job satisfaction, expedient administrative procedures, good collaborative relationships, etc. is to be achieved. In your capacity as leader, you will be particularly responsible for providing time and frameworks for the handling of such issues, but you cannot solve them on your own.

This is equally true in matters pertaining to daily operations. This is to say that leaders must be careful not to become providers of concrete solutions, thus entailing employees being retained in a profession-monopolistic approach to their work – with leaders completely failing to grasp the full implications of long-term goals and strategies, as well as the culture of their organisation.

Ask yourself:

1 How are job satisfaction surveys and workplace assessments planned in my organisation?
2 In my capacity as leader, how do I perform follow up actions?
3 How do I verbalise responsibility for job satisfaction?
4 Will I become a provider?

You Believe That Criticism Should Be Banned

You may recognise this situation:

• Scenario: You have three underperforming employees. Actually, they are also responsible for reduced standards within the rest of the team, as they generate a contagious negative atmosphere and poor quality. In fact, you feel that you ought to criticise this circumstance, but you fear that your staff will react adversely to your feedback. Also, you consider yourself to be a poor leader, if you take up a negative and critical attitude.

The appreciation wave has left many employees and leaders with the conviction that criticism is banned. The fear of criticising their employees is at the top of the list of things leaders fear most of all. This gives food for thought. In our view, criticism constitutes a crucial and necessary element in leadership. You get what you tolerate! If you tolerate an employee's poor collaborative performance, you will, at the same time, intimate that such behaviour is acceptable. This is not the first time, you hear this. Why then, are so many leaders nevertheless letting things slide? Because these leaders adhere to the overriding assumption that criticism is unacceptable. They believe that omission – i.e. refraining from calling attention to sensitive matters – means less risk of harming a relation. But instead, such leadership will give rise to new behavioural standards. Albeit unacceptable according to organisational guidelines, misconduct is tolerated in practice. And, when all is said and done, it is practice that counts.

You believe that your organisational values emphasise expectations to good behaviour. This is not the case. In your capacity as leader, it is your responsibility to communicate such behavioural standards as are expected and how they should unfold in practice. Moreover, you need to prove that you will enforce these standards in practice. But many leaders shy away from this. They will postpone or abstain from having decisive interviews with their employees. As mentioned earlier: In a survey of effective performance management, carried out on and among senior executives, 63 per cent consider their leaders' lack of courage and capability, with respect to having difficult interviews, to be their most significant challenge (Heen & Stone, 2014, p. 5). The paradox of this statement is that, frequently, the chief executives will, themselves, fail to carry out the difficult interview, to deal with their leaders' failure to carry out the difficult interviews, and to hold them responsible.

Henning Bang (2012) developed a research design for the purpose of investigating what prevents leaders in management teams from openly stating that they consider the objective of a discussion, held at a leadership team meeting, to be unclear, or that they believe the meeting to be sidetracked. One of the basic assumptions appearing most clearly among the leaders was precisely their concern that any criticism might be construed as a negative action, and that this would be problematic:

> They seemed to equate speaking up with criticising and confronting people. Ken (CEO, aged 61) said: "I'm afraid that it could be perceived as negative and arrogant, and that it would be to pinpoint a weakness. And pinpointing weaknesses is negative, right?"
>
> (Bang, 2012, p. 194)

Criticism is banned, is it not? And many leaders are afraid of others' emotional reactions:

> People might, for example, become irritated, insecure, defensive, feel rejected or embarrassed, cry or feel hurt. As Amy (VP, aged 39) told me: "I'm afraid of hurting the other [y]. Sometimes a person presents a matter that is poorly prepared, and it is too easy and facile. The quality is too low, to put it that way. But I suppose it would be offensive to say so."
>
> (Bang, 2012, p. 195)

We recently worked with the leader of an after-school care facility. The leader experienced that one team of after-school care facility teachers was not performing optimally. The approach to us had been a long time coming. At our initial interview with the leader during the start-up phase concerning the background and history, we understood that this team had been causing problems for quite some time. They went their own way, did not collaborate with their colleagues, used reproaching and negative language in their communication with parents, and often they would scold the children. We asked what actions the leader had already taken or intended to take with respect to this issue. This question triggered a longer story to the effect that, for a long time, the leader had in fact wished to tell the team about his experiences. But that to do so seemed completely wrong. Asked why, the leader plunged into a long-winded speech on appreciative leadership. This particular leader had attended a course programme that had focused comprehensively on an appreciative approach. On this background, the leader had also invited the course teachers to hold development courses for his teachers in the after-school care facility. In the leader's opinion, the culture of the after-school care facility would benefit from this as, frequently, there would be a negative atmosphere during teacher-team discussions of various shared approaches. However, the leader now had the feeling that it would appear highly incredible if, at this point, he should call attention to such behaviour as he found unacceptable. This would mean renouncing the very idea of the culture he had initiated.

All too often, organisations have ended up being dominated by discourses on appreciation, consideration, that 'no one has a monopoly on truth,' etc. No one dares to mention their experiences though, because, after all, they only represent one's personal perspective. Other people are obviously entitled to their perspectives. Albeit not the business of the systemic approach, this is unfortunately very often the consequence. Although there may be much good in appreciation and the systemic approach, it should be noticed that no culture will arise from misguided consideration.

Our point is that, when fair and reasonable, your, the leader's, criticism of your employees, their performance and behaviour is both legitimate and necessary. Similarly, we believe that peer-to-peer criticism – by peer leader to peer leader, as by peer to peer – may be called for. If a teacher observes a fellow teacher performing poor teaching, we believe that the teacher has an obligation to call attention to his observation – towards his colleague, the workplace, and the pupils. When time and again, a nurse observes a physician's carelessness and use of abusive language in connection with his examination of patients, it is the nurse's co-responsibility to criticise such behaviour.

We are duty bound to state our opinion, even though we always consider things from own perspectives, and even though we cannot claim to have a patent on truth. This is not least true for people in leadership positions. A leader failing to censure unacceptable circumstances will send the signal to employees that nothing is going to happen – that the management will refrain from coping with such unacceptable behaviour. And then the usual routines can continue, as has been the case for years.

Goffee and Jones (2006) introduce the interesting concept of 'tough empathy' which is a kind of resilient empathy. Notwithstanding the leader's experiential acknowledgement of his/her employees' experiences, the leader will not let him-/herself be controlled by such acknowledgements and, likewise, this will not have an adverse effect on the leader's capacity for using his authority, plotting a course, setting goals, and making decisions. We experience too many leaders who have let themselves become entrapped by 'soft empathy,' making themselves believe that they should take their point of departure in employees' emotions and well-being. With such a focus, the leader entirely forgets the commercial aspect. If employees' emotions and well-being become controlling factors in your leadership perception, then your chance of succeeding with your leadership task will most frequently be at a minimum.

Tough-empathy training may be an important method in your practice of fearless leadership. This mindset will legitimise your persistency, your demand-making, and your standing on your course. In this context, it is important that, subsequently, you reflect on your emotional reactions in the situation. One way of beginning to train tough empathy will be that, in concrete situations (e.g. at meetings), you raise your awareness with respect to the registration of your experiences concerning your employees' emotions and discourses, while, at the same time, you stay focused on a constant assessment of what will be the 'right' thing to do for the organisation. It must pivot on what is required and not on what you feel for. In Chapter 3, we shall discuss how tough empathy is concretely trained.

Ask yourself:

1   Which interviews have I postponed?
2   When will I curb what I think and feel?
3   When do I pussyfoot around things?
4   What is the organisational consequence of my pussyfooting?
5   How do I cope with my employees' emotions?
6   What will their emotions and attitudes trigger in me?
7   Do I permit my employees' emotions to become too controlling in my decision-making and actions?

You Do Not Care for Asymmetry

You may recognise this situation:

- Scenario: You are appointed as the new leader of the department in which you were yourself an employee. You have been on good terms with your colleagues – indeed, you were practically friends with some of them. Suddenly, you have become the leader of those with whom you used to be a colleague and a friend. You must decide who shall do what, which goals shall be set, whether quality is satisfactory, etc. Suddenly, your former colleagues no longer speak to you as much as they used to. One time, passing the staff room, you experienced an abrupt silence. They were sure to be talking about you, and this in ways they did not want you to overhear.

Tom was a head of department at a university institute with 60 employees. He had arrived from a different type of university and looked forward to new frameworks and new tasks. The staff was very competent and comprised a good mix of professors, lecturers, PhD students, administrative staff, etc. Being a former researcher, Tom had encountered management styles, which he had not found particularly constructive. His predecessor had been far too aloof and had made decisions without involving himself in everyday routines.

Tom spent his first months becoming acquainted with his new employees on a one-to-one basis. He experienced this as being really useful. He got a good impression of the staff and felt that he had succeeded in establishing good relations with the individual employees.

It was quite some time after this, that the problems first arose. Tom had been absorbed in the procurement of funds, contributed to the quality assurance of concrete papers and reports, and generally been preoccupied with securing a sound working basis. But lately, he had experienced certain employees to be going their own way – a bit too far and, also, the quality of their work was unsatisfactory. The employees in question did not actually involve their colleagues. They therefore had no other perspectives on their work and, thus became far too biased in their approaches. Moreover, the surrounding world was exerting an increasing pressure requiring more interdisciplinary work – which they did not deliver. Last, but not least, these employees did not contribute to their research teams, and hence were of no use to their team colleagues.

We discussed the situation with Tom, who came to realise that he had primarily been occupied with practical and framework-related matters. We asked him why he had refrained from dealing with the issue. He answered that he found it OK to take on the role of leader and deal with structural matters. But why should he play the part of 'nestor' to highly competent and grown-up people? Why should he be a know-all, deciding what would be the right ways to collaborate and work? How could that possibly be OK? "Because *you're* it. You're the leader," we told him.

This gave rise to a chat about Tom's understanding of his leadership role, and we drew up a set of improvement goals focused on being unequivocal, making demands, and plotting a course.

Many leaders tend to balk at the idea of taking on an asymmetrical position towards their employees. 'After all, we are all equal.' The consequence of this, however, will be a lack of direction, low standards and, typically, also too many conflicts.

The historical organisational hierarchy has, in many respects, been replaced by far more fluid organisational structures. The leader cannot always hide behind well-defined roles and descriptions. To a certain extent, the formal and obvious authority must therefore be completed by a more personal authority. Management literature (see e.g. Visholm, 2004) distinguishes between three modes of authority: authority from below (owing to acceptance and approval by employee followers (or fans)), authority from above (the formal and structural power and empowerment), and authority from within (whether a person feels empowered to exert authority). Not only will there be leaders who simply are not sufficiently authorised from above, as many leaders will also struggle with feeling authorised from within. Being authorised from within means that you experience self-respect in your dealings with other people – in the sense that you feel relaxed in such relations, feel appreciated and neither persecuted, intruded upon, nor humiliated. Authority from within is, to a considerable extent, a result of experiences with previous authorities in our lives. Experiences, that continue to affect our capacity for positioning ourselves in asymmetric relations. According to Holm (2014, p. 49, authors' translation): "In a leadership context, this means that, in his/her capacity as leader, a person who feels comfortable with having authority will, thus, have a strong capacity for entering into power-asymmetric relations – without either becoming authoritarian or prompting submissiveness."

To a leader, it is important to be able to manage oneself in one's role and, for instance, find out how one contributes with one's resources. It is important that the leader has the courage to bring his/her resources and power into play. Frequently, such courage may be affected by feelings such as envy and rivalry among employees, which may engender unpleasant emotions in leaders. In such cases, some leaders will then try to steer clear of these emotions by way of democracy and equality management. But such management will result in an undermining of the leader's authority and leadership capabilities (Obholzer, 2003).

Ask yourself:

1 Which authority figures have appeared in my life?
2 Have they in any way contributed to make me the leader I am today?
3 When do I lead the way in my capacity as leader, because I *am* a leader?

You Believe That You Must Be Confident

You may recognise this situation:

• Scenario: Your superior has announced the necessity of introducing a savings plan. The cost-saving programme is to be developed and implemented over the next three years. You communicate this to your employees, which gives rise to a number of questions from your group of employees: How comprehensive will the cost savings be? Who will be in charge of the process? Should we feel insecure? Which areas will be prioritised in the future? How will you, the leader, control the process? And so on. As the questions begin to rain down on you, you suddenly experience a feeling of incompetence. Why am I incapable of answering these questions? Do I even have a strategy?

When, for the first time ever, Mona sought coaching assistance, she was 46 years old. In fact, she considered it to be a bit embarrassing. She was the leader of a hospital unit for spinal injuries that employed a number of physiotherapists, chiropractors, and physicians. Within the unit, they had discussed their organisational and collaborative structure, and there was a growing dissatisfaction with the state of affairs. There were other issues. In the first place, their organisation into teams was inexpedient. And, secondly, their physical framework was ineffective – in particular the location of treatment rooms relative to the reception area. The employees had complained about these matters and demanded a solution. Mona had contemplated a new team structure and the possibility of moving the reception to the opposite end – closer to the entrance. She had proposed some of her ideas but had received quite diffuse feedback. There were those who considered this a very fine solution, as it would shorten the walking distance to the reception area, and team meetings would become more relevant with respect to case-management summarising. Others again found this a proposal that would only give rise to other, though similar, issues, because this way, the patients would actually have to pass through a different ward, and besides, the performance of the new teams would never be satisfactory.

Mona was giving a lengthy presentation of all her considerations, until we asked her what it would take for her to come to a decision. Well, she would of course have to be sure that her solution was a good one. She should be able to guarantee the employees that the new solution would solve some of the problems they were experiencing. Mona was truly working overtime.

To leaders, making decisions on a shaky basis constitutes one of our most major fears. Perhaps you also believe that you must be confident – that you must be able to provide answers. To analyse your overall situation and make rational decisions. To apply systematic tools. To plan carefully prepared strategies. To be in control of organisational events and minimise insecurity. Naturally, you work targeted, knowing where you and your employees are going. The predominant discourse on the sensible leader who is in control makes a set of social identities available about the leader as a rational leader who is capable of taking charge. On this background, it is hardly surprising that many leaders experience that they are required to satisfy the idea of, and present themselves as, rational leaders who are capable of applying analytical skills for the purpose of identifying solutions and of implementing carefully prepared strategies targeted at reaching organisational goals. The thing is, however, that leaders are far from always feeling confident. Thus, there is a gap between the social identity, made available by the leadership discourses, and the actual sense of identity that is, in fact, characteristic of many leaders. This may make leaders consider themselves to be awkward and poor leaders. They feel that they are not equal to the (imagined) expectations of their surroundings:

> They would all look at me in a faintly disappointed way, having expected something like leadership to light up the room. They

expected me to be confident and knowledgeable, and I was … still just me, when I needed to become a manager.

(Hay, 2014, p. 512)

Studies (Hay, 2014) show that the experience of having to match the discourse depicting the confident and strong leader is linked with considerable fear. Hay interviewed a number of leaders, who were attending a leadership course, about their experiences, benefits, etc. One of her findings was not only surprising, but also inadvertent relative to the objective of the study, as she discovered that leaders appeared to feel insecure with respect to their leadership, as they experienced that, in fact, they did not have solutions to all challenges, whereas they experienced solutions to be expected by their surroundings:

> There are also other challenges where colleagues look to me for direction, and I don't know! They are looking at me, and I don't know! So, it puts a bit of pressure on you because how you can help other people … I think deep down you do have some ideas … because it is very easy to be a bit scared and say, "I don't know what I'm doing at all here!"
>
> (Hay, 2014, p. 515)

The consequence of believing that one needs to be confident, though not *feeling* confident, may be self-deception. The discourse about the confident leader will, ironically, make it difficult for leaders to express their insecurity. In the course of time, leaders will therefore often compel themselves to believe that they are confident. At the risk of overlooking things that require action-taking, they turn a blind eye to their insecurity, because they dare not pause and raise questions as to whether they are taking the right action. Instead, they force themselves to take a unilateral view of the world. They seek such conditions and arguments as will, on the face of it, support them in their choices and assessments. And they ignore the virtual presence of ambiguity and complexity. This is how, as a leader, you may run the risk of hiding behind tools.

We do not need more self-sufficient leaders. On the contrary, leaders who dare to doubt, and not least, expose and share their doubts and insecurities, should be immensely popular. However, we almost always end up recruiting the self-assured and arrogant leaders, because they appear to be more competent. We find it difficult to reset our psychological pre-understandings, that self-assurance equals competence, and instead we focus on the fact that humble leaders may be far more competent.

Ask yourself:

1   When am I insecure?
2   What will I do about this insecurity?
3   When is it OK for me to be in doubt and feel insecure, and to com-
    municate this to my employees?
4   When am I pretending to be confident? And why?

You Shy Away from Decision-Making

You may recognise this situation:

- Scenario: On the one hand. On the other. You are in doubt. If you
  do not take action soon, there is a risk that your challenge will not
  be dealt with. Things will go from bad to worse. But, if you do
  take action, will this be the right thing to do? People around you
  are adopting a wait-and-see attitude. They are waiting. You are
  paralysed.

Terry was the owner-manager of a business which he himself
had founded. The company marketed IT solutions and electronic
learning material for the educational sector. In the course of the
first nine years, the business had undergone tremendous growth
and now employed a staff of 60 employees. Even though, in spite
of the financial crisis, the company's turnover remained fairly
stable, the company was under constant pressure, because an
increasing number of competitors had begun to enter the market
with pirated products, and the company's turnover had stagnated.

When Terry founded the company, the principal focus was
on special robots which could be applied in various educational
games. He soon employed four immensely committed and skilled
employees, and the team established at the beginning remained
unchanged. The team had, however, been complemented by a new
head of department, because Terry had restructured the company
for the purpose of ensuring development within existing business
areas. At management meetings, the new leader had repeatedly
problematised the team and their sales rates. For the past six
months, the business had been going in the wrong direction. And
things were beginning to be critical.

When we were introduced to the company, our task was to establish a shared direction and consensus in the management team.
Having witnessed the head of department's repeated comments

upon his team and observed the managing director's response, we opted for confronting the managing director with our mystification as to why he would reject the head of department's assessment without as much as inquiring further into the matter. We wondered at the managing director's arguments, which showed signs of being more historically conditioned than being ascribable to sound commercial arguments. The managing director launched into a long narrative of the four employees; of the incredible energy and commitment and hard work they had contributed since the founding; of how well he knew them personally; etc. This gave rise to an intense debate about the company's status and the leaders' worry concerning the future. And the managing director was challenged on his decision-making willingness with respect to adapting the company to the considerable change in the market. The managing director requested to have individual chats with us, and in this connection, we talked about his major fear concerning the adaptation of the organisation and of making any changes to the team, he had employed since the very beginning. In the first place, he felt that he owed them a lot; and, secondly, he very much feared the consequences of an adaptation of the product portfolio. Would he be making a mistake? Would it be an utter failure? Was the company on its way to lose its footing?

We have heard such stories before, told by many leaders, and with respect to widely different agendas. We know of one leader, who desperately needed to rearrange some employees to new offices, but who feared the consequence of this decision. Would it be the right thing to do? Would his employees continue to perform their duties just as well as before?

According to existentialist theories (see e.g. Maddi, 2004), there is considerable difference in people's tendencies: whether they go new ways or repeat old habits – whether they choose present or past. We experience leaders who have carried out the same type of management and retained an organisation in the same routines for years. In our interviews with these leaders, they will tell us that the one thing, which may prevent their restructuring, procurement of new assignments, or introduction of new initiatives, is their fear of the consequences. They feel insecure as to whether their choice will be the right one, and hence refrain from taking action. Without one answer or one objective truth, and hence one meaning of life, we may come to doubt our own beliefs and what will create value. Thus, a kind of anxiety, which existentialists refer to as an existential anxiety (Maddi, 2004), may frequently arise.

Will it lead to personal insecurity about making a decision and taking action? Maybe it will even lead to failure? In that case, they rather prefer the safe and well-known road: The road that experience has proved to be satisfactory. However, with such leadership attitudes, they risk that their organisation will stagnate or even become extinct, just as, personally, they run the risk of being left with a feeling of meaninglessness.

Maddi (2004) conducted a 12-year longitudinal study of 450 leaders. He followed the same leaders over a 12-year period, examining their behaviour and, not least, their way of coping with stressful situations. Maddi discovered that there was considerable difference in these leaders' approach to stress and that the background for this could, in particular, be found in the difference between leaders' existential courage, especially manifested as robustness and stamina, or – put more concretely: Whether the leaders' approach to occurrences was characterised by enthusiasm and commitment. Such an approach is about whether you will remain connected with the people and occurrences surrounding you, even though this may be difficult and unpleasant, and it is about whether you will continue to try to exercise an influence over your surroundings – even though this may be challenging. But it is also about whether you will challenge yourself, i.e. to which extent you will maintain an approach that is based on learning from experiences – be they positive or negative. The leaders with a high score on all these parameters were those who thus had most existential courage and who would also be best at coping with stressful situations. Consequently, they will be the ones with the best decision-making potential – also under pressure.

Other than existential anxiety, fear of decision-making may also be about fear of being humiliated and of appearing incompetent (cf. the introduction). This fear may affect leaders' way of assuming responsibility and leadership. If fear of appearing incompetent is lurking, there are leaders who will have a tendency to shirk responsibility and important decision-making. Instead, they will procrastinate, leave decision-making to others, refrain from participating in processes, and fail to take the lead. They become too dependent on other people and on other people's expectations of them. How other people feel about them. Their ability to act as independent individuals, and hence as leaders, is too weak. We shall return to the theme of independence in Chapter 3.

Ask yourself:

1   How do I experience difficult decisions?
2   How do I cope with doubt in decision-making processes?
3   How do I cope with my own insecurity in decision-making?
4   Are there areas in which I delay decisions because I fear the consequences?

5 How is my ability to take responsibility, despite my experience of considerable insecurity?
6 How is my ability to act independently? To how large an extent am I dependent on the attitudes, feelings and social norms of others?

You Believe a Heavy Workload to Be a Redeeming Factor and That Your Door Must Always Be Open

You may recognise these situations:

- Scenario 1: You hurry along from one meeting to the next. Your calendar is full, packed with meetings. You burst into the room, yanking out your iPad. You have to hasten out the door for the next meeting. You experience yourself to appear as competent, the way you are flying about. People can see how important you are.
- Scenario 2: When, once in a blue moon, you can be found in your office, working on the backlog of important cases, you leave your door open. You feel that you need to be accessible, and you have learnt that your door should always be open.

Rose-Marie was a leader of a citizen service centre in a medium-sized municipality. When we met her, Rose-Marie did, in every way, give the impression of being a tad volatile. She contacted us for the purpose of handling a team-development process for her management team and a number of employee teams.

She told us that her leaders did not really contribute or implement decisions. Also, she did not feel that the teams performed as they should. She also told us that she had previously been the head of a privately owned business for which she had organised and structured tasks, meetings, functions and roles in a much more clearly defined way. After two weeks in her new position, she had registered everything to be in a state of total chaos. Conflict levels were high, case-process descriptions were non-existent, and the teams did not coordinate their work. Though preoccupied with procedures and case processes, Rose-Marie's focus on relations and job satisfaction was considerable. She decided to initiate a process targeted at an enhancement of the social capital at the citizen service centre. She therefore organised a series of meetings and project days headed by herself. And she had interviews with all staff members about their satisfaction in their job and their role in the department. At the same time, she initiated the introduction of new systems for case processes and collaboration between teams.

When we first met Rose-Marie, she had worked in the department for two years. She told us that, in the course of this period, she had gained 15 kg and had worked 70 hours a week – since the very beginning. She and her husband had initially agreed that, during the start-up phase, he would take charge of the home front, because this position had enabled her to make a really important and exciting career move. After a period of two years, however, the pressure of work had gone from bad to worse. Asked how she managed to keep up steam, her voice faltered, but she really hoped that, this summer, she would be able to take one week of holiday. Yet, there was every indication that this would not be possible.

After our first introductory meetings, Rose-Marie requested a personal coaching process prior to the commencement of our work with the department's teams. It soon became evident that Rose-Marie had reached the end of her tether. We asked her what it would be like for her to take the desired one-week holiday and completely shut her mind to the job. Her answer came as a surprise to herself: She was afraid to do so! She was scared stiff at the thought of suddenly stopping in her tracks, check how she felt, and find out that she was at breaking point. That would be far too taxing for the department, not to mention for herself. Imagine the consequences, if she cracked up? We talked about the background for this situation, and Rose-Marie arrived at the conclusion that she had made herself too indispensable by far. She always ended up having the final responsibility, in every aspect. Her leaders took no steps without Rose-Marie being involved. And, so as to prevent politicians' complaints about the department, she insisted on being kept informed about all the leaders' responsibilities and on reading many of the decisions made by their staffs. She had practically become addicted to the snowballing effect of the velocity she had created. She always managed to explain away the considerable importance of a current situation and the necessity of her presence – to herself and to her support base. Deep down, she feared that she would not prove successful in her leadership position. That the politicians or her superior would find out that she was not in absolute control. It was this fear that, each and every day, would drive her to invest far more energy than was necessary.

The number of leaders who feel stressed out, and their nerves worn thin, is huge. A comprehensive research project (Hougaard, 2018) demonstrates that leaders are having tremendous difficulties with keeping focused and with the performance of their duties. Of the leaders included in the research, 73 per cent feel non-mindful for most of the time, 96 per cent of the responding leaders would like to be more mindful, 67 per cent of the responding leaders describe their minds as cluttered, and, as a result, 65 per cent often fail to complete their duties. According to this research, the largest sources of distraction are: demands from other people (26 per cent); competitive priorities (25 per cent); general distractions (13 per cent); and a workload that is too comprehensive (12 per cent).

Many have become completely unfocused and will perform too many tasks themselves. They perform micromanagement, and hence do not *lead*. Instead of pausing to get an overview, their only strategy will be a persistent increase in working hours. This will have fatal consequences – for the leaders themselves as for the workplaces.

It is as if those leaders fail to discover how things are on the point of falling apart at the seams. That, indeed, they 'just need to get satisfactorily over this period.' Slowly, they become entrapped in some basic assumptions, or fallacies, about their being indispensable or about how they need to perform, or control, each and every matter themselves. Thus, their 'solution' will only be a perpetual expansion of the timeframe – in order that they become enabled to get more work done.

Many leaders have learnt that it is highly commendable to practice an 'open-door policy.' And who would not want to be accessible, attentive, and helpful? Consequently, our door is left open, and the employees love us for this. The problem is, however, that the effect of the open door will also render us annoyed, non-helpful, and non-attentive. Quite concretely, the open door is responsible for at least four unfortunate factors:

1 Actually, you are not attentive. Your non-attentiveness will not only affect your ability to stay focused, it will also affect your surroundings.

2 You rob your employees of the opportunity to develop. Frequently their presentation of issues is also a matter of their professional standards, not yours. For instance, teachers should be able to cope with problems in their classes on their own. It is a matter of their professional standards, not yours. When willingly and proud, you hasten out the door to solve a conflict in a class, or a parental conflict, you will literally rob your teachers of important learning and development.

3 As a leader, you run the risk of solely being in contact with a minority of your employees, namely those who have a disruptive effect. You will ignore all those who, for various reasons, will not

disturb you, even if they might have a genuine need of seeing you, or even if you might have a genuine need to see them.

4   You lose track of the long-term and decisive strategic goals.

We are in no way advocating the idea that leaders must close their doors and solely perform leadership by way of a computer or spreadsheets. On the contrary, we are very much in support of leaders who leave their offices for the purpose of performing leadership across the entire relational field. We do, however, believe that this should take place in a more proactive and organised way. That the leaders turn their sights on their organisations and proactively decide when they consider it expedient to be present and effectively attentive. At which team meetings? In connection with which agendas? Relative to which challenges? We never get to consider these questions because we have grown into the habit of the open door, letting it control our daily routines.

As mentioned in the introduction, we all have a basic interpersonal need to feel competent. This need, combined with the fear of appearing incompetent or be humiliated, will affect our behaviour relative to the extent to which we seek to influence, control, affect, take responsibility, etc. The fear of appearing incompetent may soon trigger a self-feeding vicious circle within which you, the leader, will be running faster and faster to complete, and be on top of, things. At the same time, an inner voice warning you of your lacking overview will only become louder, and you will drive yourself to run faster and faster, because you will thus succeed in deceiving yourself into believing that you will then be effective, competent, and important.

Ask yourself:

1   How brisk is my walk when I walk down the hallway?
2   Am I aware how my brisk activity will affect my surroundings?
3   When will I close the door to actually succeed in coping with major tasks to which I need to devote my absolute attention?
4   How hectic am I?
5   Do I find it difficult to remember things, even though they may just have occurred?
6   How dependent do I believe my organisation to be on me?
7   How will my heavy workload influence my overview?
8   Do I give endless speeches?
9   Do I find it difficult to keep my temper under control?

You Believe That You Can Hide Behind Tools

You may recognise this situation:

- Scenario: One of your teams is not functioning satisfactorily. One after another, the employees are coming to see you about their problems. Their stories are especially about how they experience differences in performance. Some will experience that others are freewheeling and, also, late for work. Others again will experience certain of their colleagues to be working according to mistaken priorities. Fortunately, you have attended a course in time recording and a new planner-handling tool. For this reason, you introduce the group to these systems and ask the employees to apply this tool in order that time and tasks can be brought under control. The actual fact is that you are afraid of the grumpy old employees who are constantly criticising the newcomers for their poor performance.

A few years ago, we worked for the senior management team of a major educational institution. The organisation had only existed a few years, but because it was the result of a major merger, it was a very comprehensive organisation. The team of senior executives had come under significant pressure, externally – from politicians and the press, as well as internally – from a staff who experienced chaos and lack of support. We looked into the way the management team and senior management team engaged in leadership. It turned out that, over the past year, the senior management team had introduced six new IT systems for the purposes of providing management, order, overview, and control. The organisational effect of this was employees and mid-level managers who had become fed up with all the new concepts and systems they had to deal with and implement. Not least because, frequently, the concepts and systems could not be adapted in departments. They had, in general, been designed and implemented on the basis of a 'one size fits all' concept, which was inexpedient.

On their part, the senior management team could present valid stories substantiating that concepts and systems were outdated, and that hence the professional levels of the organisation and management needed enhancement. The upshot was that the leaders had become system administrators, and thus they failed to establish the management culture and attitude that would facilitate their handling of the complexity that characterised the organisation.

We spoke with a number of leaders at different managerial levels, and many felt a major pressure for measuring up to the 'professional' leadership concept. They had to perform, whilst they and their employees experienced an inability to cope with concrete situations in ways that were in any way useful.

Many of the leaders with whom we work, seek tools for planning, control, optimisation, administration, solutions, etc. In so far as this goes, there is nothing wrong with that. We all know the effectiveness of applying a good tool, be this a useful performance-review tool, a strategic tool, etc. The problem is attitude, if you believe that leadership can be practiced through the application of systematic tools. Today, many organisations are characterised by an immense complexity which makes it impossible to exercise this kind of leadership. The pace of change is faster than ever before: Interdisciplinary performance, distributed leadership, projects, etc. will increase the complexity within which leaders shall act and succeed each and every day. According to predominant discourse, and as already mentioned, the leaders may frequently hold the answer. They know what needs to be done. They have well-defined objectives, they practice logical leadership, and they are professional. But observing leaders in their daily practice, as the leadership thinker Henry Mintzberg did, this is not the case at all (Mintzberg, 2011). Leaders' everyday situations are characterised by considerable chaos, and their activities are action-oriented, fragmented and brief. In spite of this, however, the message of the most valid discourses on management nonetheless continue to repeat that leaders plan, organise, lead, and control.

In our experience, as also verified by various studies (Sturdy et al., 2006), leaders will feel more self-assured and bolstered in the wake of leadership courses focused on tools and new knowledge. They will brush up their theoretical knowledge on leadership, they will once again be able to demonstrate that they know a thing or two, and they will indulge in the name-dropping of the most contemporary theories and concepts. It is not so much the possible introduction of new tools that makes a difference, it is rather the self-assurance linked with keeping up with the most novel development. Because the newly acquired (or refreshed) tools will frequently lose out in a complex world, we experience that the new self-assurance often stands on a fragile foundation. Anxiety is lying in wait. Who has participated in a more novel or more popular course? Can I be sure that my tools really are the most recent and the best? Etc. We experience that leaders who demonstrate much self-assurance may feel an even greater extent of anxiety than those leaders who are not necessarily as self-assured, because the former will very often experience that they have much more at stake.

Anxiety is in hot pursuit of complexity. Ralph Stacey, one of the most highly rated complexity theorists, describes (see e.g. Stacey, 2012) how groups encompassed by complexity may respond with uncertainty and anxiety and, also, how this may lead to considerable dependency on the leader who is expected to be ready with an answer. On his/her part, the leader may be nudged into a desire for dealing 'professionally' with things and will therefore apply professional tools. Often, the tools will not capture the complexity, though.

The discourse on the confident and dynamic leader engenders both employees' and peer leaders' expectations for drive and confidence. This will create a pressure for action that will typically make the leader act on the basis of competences and thoroughly tested methods rather than taking action relative to what is needed. The leader runs the risk of turning a blind eye to his uncertainty. This will obstruct new decision-making that will allow for the complexity, and hence the flexibility, that is so much in demand in a complex world.

Leaders often grumble about employees who demonstrate resistance to change. Resistance to change is frequently construed as the reason for the failure of change. But the leaders forget to bring themselves into the equation and realise how change may be curbed by their own behaviour. Thus, exposing oneself, one's uncertainties, doubt, and fear may generate an incredible anxiety. Instead, the leaders will deceive themselves into believing that they know all and are in control of things. We sometimes speak with leaders about how supportive it can be to feel confident. It is a feeling you can almost be high on. Playing for safety will, however, limit leadership work significantly. To some leaders this may for instance result in excessive management by rules, description of functions and procedures, etc., which will typically leave an organisation in a state of paralysis.

Ask yourself:

1 How often will I resort to concrete tools in coping with my day-to-day challenges?
2 What is my reason for this?
3 Will I sometimes be chasing management tools, rather than use my own judgement?
4 What might I fear by taking a more direct approach to my challenges, without being able to control the outcome?

You Consider Vulnerability a Weakness

You believe that as a leader you must be confident, strong, knowledge-able, able to cope with everything, and have an answer to everything. You will, perhaps unconsciously, adopt this position of the strong leader that is made available by the discourse. But leadership is no exact discipline with unequivocal and conclusive answers. Provided that you are in contact with your body and your emotions, you may often experience doubt, uncertainty, and fear. Maybe such feelings make you believe that you are weak. Your ego will not take kindly to this. It is writhing in agony. You hide your vulnerabilities because you fear social punishment, namely that others will consider you incompetent and weak.

When you hide your vulnerability, you contribute to the creation of a performance culture in which everyone around you is much more preoccupied with making a good impression than with their own development. A culture in which your employees and peer leaders will hide their imperfections and insecurities – in which no one dares to take risks, and everyone is entrapped in an unhealthy perfectionism. And to which you therefore contribute by bringing about a reduction in the rate of learning.

Vulnerability is the road towards courage. You cannot be courageous without being vulnerable. When we hear the word vulnerability, we often mistakenly confuse the term with fragile. However, vulnerability is a universally human feeling that occurs when we find ourselves in difficult situations that are characterised by uncertainty, risk, and emotional exposure (Brown, 2018). This is a state of mind we all experience. If you act in a situation that does not entail any fear or discomfort to you, you are not acting courageously. Because, in that case, the situation did not require any courageousness on your part. Vulnerability is equal to having the courage to position yourself in, and remain in, the emotional discomfort that a certain situation will release in you – and it is about acting in such ways as the situation will require. You may, for instance, cope with a conflict, ask for help, be open about finding something to be difficult, etc. And the vulnerability constitutes your openness about also experiencing fear, uncertainty, doubt, and mistakes.

Ryan was the head of the HR department of a medium-sized Danish company. Even as a newly qualified, he had relatively soon gained a good reputation within the trade because of his cleverly worded articles and his contribution to the setting of professional standards. Prior to his current position, he had held three positions within consultancy, and here he had always been highly respected for his professional standards. He was now occupying a managerial position and in charge of 15 consultants of various professional backgrounds, albeit all worked within management and organisational development. He was proud of this appointment which was the job of his dreams: He had a leading position and was still occupied within his discipline. Nonetheless, he was becoming increasingly uncertain. Both with respect to the projects for which he was the performing consultant and with respect to his leadership of his consultants who, in many ways, tended to place him on a pedestal. Unconsciously, Ryan experienced a performance pressure in connection with having to meet their high expectations of him. However, his ego grew by the day – which had been the case throughout all the years. Every time he was praised, his ego would grow; and hence it became increasingly easier to hit the bull's eye. But the other side of coin was that Ryan could never give the game away and disclose his vulnerability. He always had to know the answers – also in cases when he did not. When his projects did not turn out to perfection, he would hide this – or criticise the internal client. This behaviour inadvertently affected the entire group of consultants to whom it also became increasingly difficult to ask for help or expose any uncertainty or mistake. And as to Ryan' own performance, this grew from bad to worse, as – rather than enable the success and development of his employees – he became more preoccupied with polishing his image so as to appear perfect in the eyes of his clients and employees. It was not until, after three years in the position Ryan struck up a conversation with a good old colleague, that he became aware of the pattern within which he had become entrapped. And it should be a long process for Ryan. Not only would he have to get in touch with and abide by his vulnerability, he would also have to engage in open communication about it. He very much had to come to terms with the fear that his associates would consider him weak and incompetent. Their responses provided food for thought, though: Everyone experienced him as more human, more competent (because he was able to reflect on himself in his capabilities as leader and consultant, and) because he would take the lead with respect to the creation of a learning culture within which people would dare to be open about their weaknesses and fallibility.

References

Amos, B., & Klimoski, R. (2014). Courage: Making Teamwork Work Well. *Group & Organization Management, 39*(1), 110–128.

Bang, H. (2012). What Prevents Senior Executives from Commenting upon Miscommunication in Top Management Team Meetings? *Qualitative Research in Organizations and Management: An International Journal, 7*(2), 189–208.

Brown, B. (2018). *Dare to Lead: Brave Work, Tough Conversations, Whole Hearts.* New York: Random House.

Goffee, R., & Jones, G. (2006). *Why Should Anyone Be Led by You? What It Takes To Be an Authentic Leader.* Boston, MA: Harvard Business School.

Hay, A. (2014). 'I Don't Know What I am Doing!': Surfacing Struggles of Managerial Identity Work. *Management Learning, 45*(5), 509–524.

Heen, P., & Stone, D. (2014). *Thanks for the Feedback: The Science and Art of Receiving Feedback Well.* New York, NY: Viking/The Penguin Group.

Holm, I. (2014). *Det personlige lederskab.* København: Hans Reitzels Forlag.

Hougaard, R. (2018). *The Mind of the Leader: How to Lead Yourself, Your People, and Your Organization for Extraordinary Results.* Boston, MA: Harvard Business Review.

Kirkeby, O. F. (1998). *Ledelsesfilosofi.* Frederiksberg: Samfundslitteratur.

Kristensen, T. (2008). Er det virksomheden, der er patienten? *Tidsskrift for ARBEJDSliv, 10*(4), 109–113.

Maddi, S. R. (2004). Hardiness: an Operationalization of Existential Courage. *Journal of Humanistic Psychology, 44*(3), 279–298.

Mintzberg, H. (2011). *Managing.* Berrett-Koehler.

Obholzer, A. (2003). Authority, power and leadership. In A. Obholzer & V. Z. Roberts (eds.). *The Unconscious at Work.* Taylor and Francis.

Schutz, W. (2005). *The Human Element: Productivity, Self-Esteem, and the Bottom Line.* San Francisco, CA: Jossey-Bass.

Stacey, R. (2012). *Tools and Techniques of Leadership and Management. Meeting the Challenge of Complexity.* Abingdon: Routledge.

Sturdy, A., Brocklehurst, M., Winstanley, D., et al. (2006). Management as a (Self) Confidence Trick: Management Ideas, Education and Identity Work. *Organization, 13*(6), 841–860.

Visholm, S. (2004). Autoritetsrelationen. In T. Heinskou & S. Visholm (eds.). *Psykodynamisk organisationspsykologi – på arbejde under overfladen.* København: Hans Reitzels Forlag.

3 The Development of Fearless Management

You cannot be afraid of dogs if you know nothing about dogs. If you have absolutely no knowledge of planes, you cannot be afraid of flying. It is just the same with knowledge of own capacities in respect of authority in interaction with other people within asymmetrical power relations – it needs to be achieved through experience rather than reading (Holm, 2014, p. 22).

Courageousness cannot be studied. This book will not make you more courageous. But you can train yourself to become more courageous. Many leadership-course programmes fail to provide adequate incorporation of the personal dimension in management. Without the personal dimension the scope will be too narrow, or participants will not get sufficient training. When management courses work with the personal dimension, this takes place in secure environments and disconnected from the leaders' everyday routines. Frequently, it will be an 'arm's length' theoretical focus. It is fine to learn *about* the personal leadership, but it is important that you work *with* this and train it. Hiding behind leadership theories or tools may feel supportive. But if you try to express the aspect of being in contact with other people by a formula, you will miss out on the aspect of your authenticity.

Though leadership programmes may touch upon the subject of courage and perhaps even stress its importance, this is a subject that cannot be taught – not by case studies, nor by simulation. The only way to test courageousness is to require that people take a leap in the dark and test themselves and their courage in real-life uncomfortable situations. Situations in which they draw on innate courage and learn to come to terms with the sensations involved (Bregman, 2013).

Over the last ten years, we have developed various ways of thinking about and developing personal leadership. Our foremost experiences are that personal leadership must take its point of departure in the individual leader and the individual leader's practice. At the best of times, directly in practice, alternatively with the point of departure in practice. In this chapter, we will describe some of the concrete approaches and methods we believe to be particularly applicable in the work with strengthening your personal leadership and your courage.

Vulnerability Courage

As mentioned, the high degrees of complexity and unpredictability, of today's world as of employees' professional skills and commitment, mean that leaders will not engage in good leadership by being heroic. Leaders must rather have the courage to be vulnerable. As indicated, vulnerability should not be confused with weakness, which is so often the case. Vulnerability is a feeling that arises when we find ourselves in difficult situations that we cannot control, situations that leave us emotionally exposed. To clear away misunderstandings, we have invented the term 'vulnerability courage' which should, preferably, emphasise that it is a matter of having the courage to feel and show our vulnerability.

To become a more courageous leader, your very first move is to accept that courage is accompanied by vulnerability. As already mentioned: A heroic action without fear and discomfort is not courageous. You must accept that uncomfortable feelings are a part of life and a part of the leadership profession. We often hear leaders say, 'but it's not very nice behaviour to have to….' But then again, 'nice' was never an element in the job specification.

Basically, when you have come to terms with this and realised that to behave more courageously you need to be more willing to embrace every emotion and not just the nice ones, this will be when you will be ready to begin your training, and not before. The next step is to initiate action learning, because it requires more than insight and acceptance to become courageous. It must be trained.

Action Learning

To build courage in leadership, we frequently use the action-learning method. This applies to the master's education programmes and in our daily work with executive development. The application of the action-learning method means that a person will develop and learn by the actual performance of something in his/her everyday routines and subsequently reflect upon this. Your learning will be most effective when you cope with real problems in their real contexts. When, in our leader coaching, we work with leaders who want to develop their managerial courage and strength, we therefore cooperate on finding real challenges that will require managerial courage. Thus, the action learning has a dual focus: You must cope with a concrete task/situation/challenge, and you will develop reflection upon your actions and the effect thereof. This method is incredibly powerful in the development of leadership competences and strengths. Many leaders experience it to be really useful to have their development systematised and to plan quite concrete actions that are targeted at coping with a situation, and yet generate learning and personal development.

We were recently contacted by a leader, Owen, who had been in his position as a leader for a year and a half. He told us that he had inherited a dysfunctional team that had been characterised by conflicts for a period of three years. One employee had already been discharged, before Owen had taken up his position, and Owen' superior was currently performing an interview process with another employee. Owen, who was very eager to believe the best of everybody, was certain that a solution could be found. But the situation did not improve. The team continued to fight over projects, communication among them was poor, they generated a negative atmosphere, refused to help one another, and there was backstabbing. Owen asked for help to design a process for his team that was aimed at resolving this conflict.

We had a heart-to-heart with Owen who admitted that he feared the employees' reactions. He was afraid they would experience that he was putting them under pressure. And he was afraid that he would not be able to cope with their anger towards each other. He was afraid that he himself 'lacked the tools' for coping with the situation. We agreed to equip him for coping with the conflict on his own. In a coaching process we worked with his emotions and courage, using action learning for training his conflict-resolution competences and, not least, his stamina and resilience capacities. Owen went to work.

In the course of the coaching sessions, the leader himself designed a sequence of meetings with conflict on the agenda. He was working at developing a methodical approach. And, not least, he was working out how to cope with himself and his fear. The employees responded with fear and frustration. Owen held his ground and insisted on putting the conflict on the agenda. The team had many tough discussions. And, at the beginning, Owen found participation at these meetings very uncomfortable: 'It is as if I'm a silhouette of myself.' He felt himself worn thin.

Owen video-recorded himself at the meetings and brought the videos to the subsequent coaching sessions. We used the videos as a common frame of reference in our discussions of what had happened at the meetings, how the leader had acted and what had been the effect of this. Owen spoke of and reflected upon concrete episodes that had been difficult. It was on this background that we developed new methods for the continuing process as well as new ways for how Owen should handle himself at the following meetings. When we concluded the coaching and action-learning process, the team was back on track, and Owen had, at the same time, become more courageous and believed more in himself. According to him, it was "So powerful. My body is roaring. It is as if drawing a sketch of oneself with a darker pencil. I feel strong, distinct, and competent."

One concrete method for getting started on action learning may proceed along the following lines:

1 Find one of the most significant challenges in your job right now. Is there anything that does not work right? Anything that would improve if you dealt with it? In this connection, consider the development that would be required if you were to meet this challenge. This could for instance be that you will become more capable of decisive action. You can also apply the calendar method, where – every Friday – you look one week ahead and seek concrete contexts in which you can train such sides of yourself that you intend to improve. Whichever method is chosen, it would be optimal for you to perform 4–5 actions a week. This sounds of much, but actually it will only require a little extra time as it is about psyching yourself up to such activities that you are already scheduled to be a part of.
2 Initiate actions. Plan your performance of a number of concrete actions targeted at dealing with the challenge you have set up. Actions that, at the same time, will contribute to your training.
3 Study yourself and your surroundings. How do you experience this? Which thoughts and feelings will arise?
4 Analyse your observations. Reflect upon what you have experienced. What is characteristic of your own reactions and those of others? Which consequences did your actions entail? What did you learn from your observations?
5 Plan new acts/actions.

In relation to this method, it is important to remember that the reference to 'actions' is not about major processes, it is about concrete actions in your everyday routines, such as for instance: 'I intend my introduction at the next leader meeting to be about increased clarity with respect to purpose and method.'

Find Your Leader Vision

As mentioned in the introduction, it is important to be able to engage in visionary leadership to extents that will generate the backing of followers, fans. Many leaders will, however, become too far removed from their leader visions in their daily routines. Thus, they will not have their visions as compass and inner engine when they find themselves in difficult leader-related circumstances.

Anya is the educational leader at an upper secondary school. At the commencement of her coaching course, Anya tells us about a teaching staff that are solely preoccupied with counting hours and their own disciplines and timetables and, also, they frequently display a critical attitude towards the management. According to Anya's observations, the teachers are non-cooperative and only take responsibility for their own teaching. And for this reason, many disciplinary processes are not properly coordinated. The teachers neither take responsibility for the environment in their classes nor for students who feel unhappy or deliver poor perform-ance. The school has performed staff satisfaction surveys which reveal that the teachers do not have much confidence in each other and that they lack recognition, by one another as by the manage-ment. Several times, Anya and her peers in the management group have tried to speak with the teachers, raising the matter of the necessity of cooperation and coordination, and – not least – the necessity of shared sparring and knowledge-sharing. Anya was getting dragged down, and she was overworking.

Rather than commencing a sparring on the situation as such, we asked Anya why she had, at all, chosen to become a leader. What was her personal story about why she was where she was? On behalf of the school, which impression would she be proud of the school having made on the young people? This spurred a long narrative, with Anya growing increasingly intense and enthusi-astic. She discovers why she has become a leader in the first place, which hopes she entertains for the development of the young people, and how these hopes link to her own past, to her youth and, in particular, to one secondary-school teacher who has meant everything with respect to Anya's education and further path in life. Anya realises the scale of the responsibility they have as a school, and she recognises how important it is to her, personally, that the school assumes this responsibility. In extension of this, it becomes clear to Anya why she actually bothers to invest so much energy in going to work and in being a leader. It also becomes clear to her what her vision commands her to do with respect to her leadership, namely that she has to discuss the necessity of collaboration with the teachers and, also, why this is of importance for the students. She will need to collar those teachers who withdraw into themselves or generate a negative atmosphere – because the current circumstances clearly have a negative impact on the students.

In her case, it was Anya's personal perception of her vision that made the pendulum swing in favour of taking the difficult interviews, of showing the way of her vision and having the courage to communicate this and stand her ground with respect to collaboration.

Thus, having one's inner vision explicated to oneself, and keeping it close to heart, constitutes an important engine in leadership work. Many leaders tend to forget the citizen/client/customer completely, in favour of an overweight of quick fixes, and they end up by solely focusing on organisation and problem solving. When we ask leaders what they consider to be important with respect to the citizen/client/customer, we very often get the response that, 'we don't really give this aspect much thought, any longer.' And this is a catastrophe. Because with the disappearance of our inner vision, and hence the invisibility of the organisational vision, this aspect will be precisely the aspect that will suddenly have been replaced by heaps of other requirements. Focus on the core task will slide. The shared passion and ethics with respect to the citizen/client/customer will water down. Egotism will begin to take over.

Exercise:

For a start, try to reflect carefully on the following – perhaps you could ask one of your peers to ask elaborating questions:

Imagine that, at some point, you are having a conversation with your child (or another person close to you). Which aspect would you be proud to communicate about your work as a leader – about what it has contributed to the life of your employees, or with respect to your citizens/students/clients/customers)?

Which difference in the world (e.g. of the workplace) would you like to take responsibility for having made?

Managing Your Immunity to Change

Together with the leaders we coach, we will sometimes discover that they will repeatedly return to a coaching session, with the words, 'Well, I did set myself these goals for personal development, but I never really got down to getting started.' They have arrived at important development areas within which they really want to make a move, and yet they procrastinate. We have become aware of an approach which has helped us and the leaders to make progress. This approach is called 'immunity to change' (Kegan & Lahey, 2009). It is a method that has been developed on the basis of observations of similar examples of failure to act (e.g. patients who must take medication – they could be patients who need to take medication, because otherwise they will die, and yet they neglect to take the prescribed medication, disregarding the facts that, in the first place, the medicine is necessary for their survival and, secondly, there are no side effects). What researchers have discovered here is that, frequently, a kind of immunity to change will occur in situations where people ignore own resolutions. It is a bit similar to comparing our physical immune defence system with a psychological immune defence mechanism that exists to protect us by way of retaining our opinion-creation system, our way of understanding the world. Just as our physical immune defence mechanism has a decisive function which may at times reject new substances that are important to our continued health, we will sometimes experience that a psychological immune defence may in similar ways prevent us from developing our understanding of things and, generally, from our development in new directions. Immunity to change is about how in addition to a speeder, i.e. what we wish to develop, we also have a brake, i.e. the competing psychological goals intended to protect us against anxiety.

Immunity to change is thus our anxiety-coping system according to which we seldom feel fear. The leader who would like to listen more – be more attentive, who, rather than using all the fine tools for listening that she has access to, will interrupt, be the first to take the word, etc., may have a competing goal about not appearing faint, vague, insecure. Here, all the leader's preventive actions to check herself – stepping on the brake – originate in an immune defence mechanism targeting the fear linked with appearing insecure, etc. What is specific about this approach is the fact that researchers have uncovered what is behind the foot on the brake, namely these competing goals that prevent our development. We therefore need to uncover these goals. An example from our work:

A leader had a desire to develop his authority, comprising his ability, at meetings, to take over procedure management and steer the meetings to successful completion. This leader further desired to set the course and establish the frameworks of the meetings. He had decided on a method for addressing the meetings according to which he would steer through the meetings, using a set of process-management tools; and, otherwise, he would make a clear appearance. However, the leader repeatedly caught himself practicing a behaviour that actually prevented him from developing within the required areas. Time and time again, the leader succeeded in convincing himself that it would be better to let the meetings progress along more loosely defined lines and 'deal with things in the dialogue.' Using the 'immunity to change' approach, the leader realised that he had a set of competing goals about being accommodating and attentive, about leaving space for everybody and not 'take up space.' It also became clear to the leader that he had a set of linked basic assumptions that told him that his potential development of authority and his making a more distinct appearance would mean running the risk of being rejected and excluded.

If you wish to identify your immunity to change, you can begin by asking yourself what you would like to introduce as a change in your work to render you more effective and satisfied (e.g. preventing meetings from being so boring and ineffective)? Then consider the values/goals that constitute the basis of what you would like to change (e.g.: I find it important that we are focused and reach our goals). To pinpoint your improvement goal, your next step will be to consider your own share of the situation being as it is (that meetings are ineffective). You could therefore ask yourself about what you do, respectively do not do, to cause an obstruction of your values (e.g.: I don't take control). This way, you arrive at your improvement goal (e.g. to take more control). In order to identify your competing goals more specifically, your next question to yourself could be whether you register any concern that is linked with your desisting from the behaviour that obstructs your development (e.g.: If I take control, I worry about being ignored by my employees, or that the others will not take an interest in the meeting). By looking into what your inexpedient behaviour could possibly prevent from taking place, you will thus arrive at the resulting competing value/goal (e.g. that my colleagues will neither be uncommitted nor ignore me). Finally, you can uncover your basic, or big, assumptions by considering what you suspect would happen if you actually commenced the development of your improvement goals (e.g.: If I take more control, and my employees ignore me or appear uncommitted, this is because I'm being rejected and because they don't like me).

Try to use the Figure 3.1, which we typically use together with our leaders, for purposes of uncovering your own immunity to change.

1. Visible Commitment	2.Doing/Not Doing Instead	3.Hidden Competing Commitments	4.Big Assumptions

Figure 3.1 Measuring immunity to change. (Kegan & Lahey, 2009). Reprinted by permission of Harvard Business Review Press. From *Immunity to Change - How to Overcome It and Unlock the Potential in Yourself and Your Organization* by Robert Kegan & Lisa L. Lahey (2009). Boston, MA. Page 57. Copyright © 2009 by the Harvard Business Publishing. All rights reserved.

The insight into competing values and the basic assumptions about what will happen if leaders succeed in their development is only a first step. It takes training to change one's view of the world. As a next step, leaders must therefore plan a series of minor actions (test actions) targeted at testing their assumptions and anxieties. At this stage, leaders will typically discover that their assumptions and anxieties are (partly) unfounded, and subsequently they will become empowered to overcome their resistance and barriers in order to succeed with the improvement goal they set themselves with respect to change. The leader of the above case realised that, admittedly, some of the employees considered the changed meeting culture to be a bit annoying, but – by and large – he was accepted in his role, without being excluded.

Emotional Intelligence

Emotional intelligence (EI) is a crucial parameter in the context of effective leadership. We live in an age of emotions in which emotions exert an incredible influence on job satisfaction and effectiveness. Competent leaders will admit to emotions in themselves and in their environment, and they can make use of such emotions in their everyday navigation. Emotions constitute pivotal data in one's interactions with one's self and with others. They communicate what is at stake, for us as for others, and they thus provide us with information about some of the absolutely crucial backgrounds for our own behaviour and that of others. We may try to ignore emotions, but this will not make them go away. This corresponds to what we referred to as defence mechanisms in the above, and – as mentioned – it emphasises that the repression of emotions comes at a price. It is expensive in terms of energy, which is removed from our presence and attentiveness – our capacity for listening and coping with situations. We may also try to hide them, but – as the attentive reader will long since have discovered – this is not an option.

Emotional intelligence is most frequently defined as a series of emotional and social skills that will determine our capacity for comprehending and expressing ourselves, our capacity for developing and retaining relations, our capacity for coping with challenges, and our capacity for applying emotional information in a meaningful way.

According to Daniel Golemann (Golemann et al., 2002) emotional intelligence is thus characterised by:

- Self-awareness
- Self-management
- Social awareness
- Relationship management

Thus, there is a self-dimension and a dimension concerned with one's coping with own relations and with one's surroundings. According to this approach, both are decisive for a leader's effectiveness.

Self-awareness is about your ability to recognise and understand your emotions. When, attending the staff meeting, you get immensely annoyed and frustrated because of your employees' failure to contribute actively, you recognise these emotions and are able to reflect upon the way they affect your behaviour and personality at the given moment. You recognise the effect your emotions will thus have on your employees.

Your *self-management* signifies your way of managing and communicating your emotions in practice. This is not to say that you cope with these emotions by suppression but, rather, that you cope with them by consciously integrating them in your decisions and actions in ways that correspond with your intensions for the situation. If, in the situation with the employees, your goal is that the employees try to understand your perspective and your agenda, you will not manage your emotions particularly well if you repress or, for that matter, give full reign to these emotions. Instead, you may perhaps manage them constructively by communicating your experience, your needs, and your requirements. You do so in a friendly yet firm manner.

Your *social awareness* might be slightly comparable to what we refer to as empathy, i.e. your ability to recognise and understand other people's emotions. Why are your employees reacting the way they are?

How is the atmosphere at the meeting? In the department? Your recognition of your employees' emotional state is a decisive factor relative to the way you cope with the management of your employees.

Relationship management is about how you transform your self-awareness and social awareness into behaviour that will bolster your relations to the effect that you will not dissociate yourself from other people, and yet you will not submit to the control of others' emotions, either. You will, however, recognise attendant emotions and the way these emotions will affect the experience of what you are preoccupied with, as well as the thoughts that will be triggered in this respect. A good leader is capable of creating and supporting such emotions as will contribute to the support of the development of current focus. This may for instance be emotions such as seriousness or enthusiasm.

A number of tools are available for work with the development of emotional intelligence. Among those, we set great store by one in particular, viz. EQ-i 2.0,[1] which is a frame of understanding and testing for assessment of the following five factors:

- Self-perception – Understand your emotions
- Self-expression – Express your emotions
- Interpersonal – Develop and maintain your relations
- Decision-making – Apply emotions in the enhancement of decision-making
- Stress management – Cope with stress

These five areas constitute an elaboration of the basic themes set out in the above. Self-perception is, for instance, also about believing in oneself and about the ability to develop one's skills and talents; whereas self-expression is also about the capacity for assertiveness and the ability to stand on one's own feet. Figure 3.2 comprises an overview of these themes.

Each theme has its own significance relative to fearless leadership; and hence the objects, on which we focus together with the leaders we are coaching, may vary considerably, albeit a few of the elements will be of more substantial significance, comprising self-acceptance, or self-regard, which is a constituent of self-perception. Self-acceptance is about respecting and accepting who we are. It is about valuing own strengths and facing up to weaknesses while, at the same time, basically respecting and accepting oneself. Self-acceptance is linked with inner strength and a belief in oneself. Inasmuch as self-acceptance is a matter of knowing own strengths and weaknesses, self-acceptance is also typically linked with a person's capacity for being sufficiently courageous to openly acknowledge own errors and, similarly, recognise that one does not have all the answers (Stein & Book, 2011).

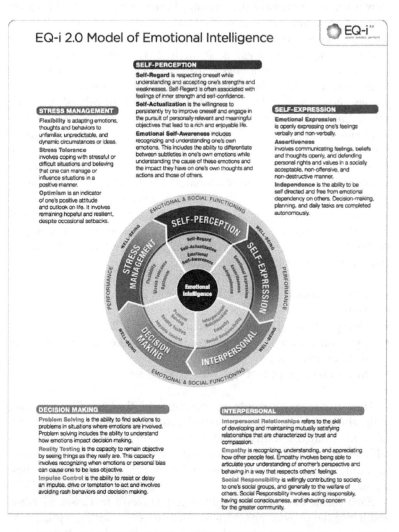

EQ-i 2.0 Model of Emotional Intelligence

SELF-PERCEPTION

Self-Regard is respecting oneself while understanding and accepting one's strengths and weaknesses. Self-Regard is often associated with feelings of inner strength and self-confidence.

Self-Actualization is the willingness to persistently try to improve oneself and engage in the pursuit of personally relevant and meaningful objectives that lead to a rich and enjoyable life.

Emotional Self-Awareness includes recognizing and understanding one's own emotions. This includes the ability to differentiate between subtleties in one's own emotions while understanding the cause of these emotions and the impact they have on one's own thoughts and actions and those of others.

STRESS MANAGEMENT

Flexibility is adapting emotions, thoughts and behaviors to unfamiliar, unpredictable, and dynamic circumstances or ideas.

Stress Tolerance involves coping with stressful or difficult situations and believing that one can manage or influence situations in a positive manner.

Optimism is an indicator of one's positive attitude and outlook on life. It involves remaining hopeful and resilient, despite occasional setbacks.

SELF-EXPRESSION

Emotional Expression is openly expressing one's feelings verbally and non-verbally.

Assertiveness involves communicating feelings, beliefs and thoughts openly, and defending personal rights and values in a socially acceptable, non-offensive, and non-destructive manner.

Independence is the ability to be self directed and free from emotional dependency on others. Decision-making, planning, and daily tasks are completed autonomously.

DECISION MAKING

Problem Solving is the ability to find solutions to problems in situations where emotions are involved. Problem solving includes the ability to understand how emotions impact decision making.

Reality Testing is the capacity to remain objective by seeing things as they really are. This capacity involves recognizing when emotions or personal bias can cause one to be less objective.

Impulse Control is the ability to resist or delay an impulse, drive or temptation to act and involves avoiding rash behaviors and decision making.

INTERPERSONAL

Interpersonal Relationships refers to the skill of developing and maintaining mutually satisfying relationships that are characterized by trust and compassion.

Empathy is recognizing, understanding, and appreciating how other people feel. Empathy involves being able to articulate your understanding of another's perspective and behaving in a way that respects others' feelings.

Social Responsibility is willingly contributing to society, to one's social groups, and generally to the welfare of others. Social Responsibility involves acting responsibly, having social consciousness, and showing concern for the greater community.

Figure 3.2 EQ-i 2.0 – Model of emotional intelligence. (Stein & Book, 2011). Reproduced with permission through PLSclear. From *The EQ Edge Emotional Intelligence and Your Success* by Stewen J. Stein & Howard E. Book (2011). Copyright ©2011 by John Wiley, Mississauga, Ontario.

Independence is another skill that is also more basic relative to fearless leadership. In our decision-making, independence is precisely about being self-contained and independent of others' feelings. Independence thus reflects the fact that, contrary to being too dependent on the expectations of our surroundings and to being trapped in 'the socialised mind' we described in Chapter 1, a person is capable of independent decision-making. Dependent persons are driven by fear. Fear of making mistakes, fear of humiliation, fear of disapproval, and fear of feeling even more useless than before (Stein & Book, 2011).

Contrary to IQ, EI can be trained and developed. For some time, we and a number of leaders have focused on the development of elements in their emotional intelligence. Relative to fearless leadership, this may frequently be concerned with impact and independence as well as flexibility in connection with the many complex, and changeable agendas. As another option, you may try to widen the gap between your emotions and your reactions so as to cope with your spontaneous emotional reactions. To begin with, this can be extremely difficult because our emotions are concretely programmed to make us react spontaneously and unconsciously. With extensive training, however, it is possible to modify our neural wiring, and hence our emotions and reactions. Very often, it starts off with the practicing of one's proficiency in becoming conscious about own emotional reactions and discovering the ways in which they make themselves felt relative to our experience of a situation and our reaction to this situation.

Focus in your training will naturally depend on which elements in the emotional intelligence you intend to train. In our training work, we generally operate with a log in which, over a period of some weeks or months, you will enter observations and experiences. In the following, we will go through a few examples of methods we have applied together with leaders with a desire for developing their emotional intelligence.

Elements in the training of your emotional intelligence could for instance be:

1 Psyche yourself up to a number of concrete situations in which you mentally prepare yourself for observing your emotions. At this early stage, you will already be able to activate your prefrontal cortex which helps you to manage your reactions. This method may benefit most factors within EI.

2 Use a logbook. Establish left-right columns. In the left column you write down your experiences of what happened. In the right column, you write down your emotions. You will be astonished at what you read about your emotions when, after the passage of a few weeks, you return to this column. At this point, you will typically not even remember that you felt like this. But you did! Incidentally, this method may, in fact, be useful with respect to most EI-related factors.

3 Try to understand your emotional reactions. What is behind? Reflect upon your reactions and be genuinely curious as to the source from which they originate and how they affect your actions. This is a

method that can be applied in and after concrete situations, and it may for instance be particularly well suited for practicing your self-perception.

4 Seek feedback on how your surroundings experience your reactions. Ask specific employees or peer leaders to observe your behaviour and the impact your behaviour has on the situation. This method may strengthen your self-perception and your self-expression and, in the long run, your ability to strengthen your relations.

5 Decide how you intend to manage your emotions in new and more constructive ways, in concrete situations. Mentally prepare yourself for registering your emotions and incorporate a 'break,' i.e. a minor lag in time during which you will have time for reflection rather than action. It is during this break that you will have time to consider what you actually want from this situation. This method is particularly efficient with respect to the strengthening of your self-control.

Mindfulness

Mindfulness is an important and highly concrete method for managing one's fear and strengthening one's emotional intelligence. As we have dealt with in the above, the ability to manage stress and emotions in leadership is becoming increasingly important. There is a growing tendency for leaders to lose their way and lose contact with themselves, and hence also the opportunities to make more well-considered and qualified leadership decisions. As previously described, many leaders are too overworked and allow their heavy workload to be contagious. One way to assess this concretely is that, at meetings, leaders are easily distracted, disturbed, stressed out, inattentive, and absent-minded. As a contrast to this, imagine a leader who – perfectly composed and calm – enters the room, sits down calmly, and opens the meeting by observing two minutes' silence, whereupon he/she is attentive towards all meeting participants. This is where mindfulness comes to your assistance. Likewise, mindfulness may help you to spot, and hence apply the brake relative to your 'amygdala-hijack' responses – the circumstances in which your emotions will take complete control and, for instance, react violently.

We construe mindfulness as the basic experience of the here-and-now awareness of the stirrings that are taking place in our physical, emotional, or mental states. It is thus a special way of being in the world in which a person is concretely in contact with oneself and one's reaction. Therefore, mindfulness is also a concrete method according to which you can achieve increased control of your emotional reactions while also providing enhanced freedom of choice in your interpersonal relations. Mindful leadership signifies a frame of mind in which we can be focused, attentive, and curious, as well as more intentional in our approach and decisions. Last, but not least, mindfulness may contribute to an increase in your self-consciousness. Qualities in management that we consider to be absolutely crucial, these days.

We primarily use mindfulness for two types of development in leadership: coping with fear and coping with stress (and associated inattentiveness and uncertainty). Mindfulness can be a tremendously powerful tool in coping with fear. By way of mindfulness, it is feasible to link fear scenarios with new bodily sensations. In general, the experience of fear will activate an array of bodily sensations. We will experience rapid heartbeat and muscular tension, and our pupils will be dilated, etc. Our body is preparing for a fight or flight behaviour. This is how we humans are programmed. The problem is that, when today, we are experiencing the release of fear, we will, in fact, neither benefit from fight- nor flight-preparedness when fear is released. Especially not in matters pertaining to leadership. On the contrary, these situations claim courage to remain calm and handle the situation in an orderly manner. Here, mindfulness exercises can link the visualisation of the fear scenarios with calm bodily reactions. It is our experience that, in the course of a few months and assisted by a variety of guided apps,[2] you will already have established a set of new and more expedient bodily reactions for underpinning a more courageous management of situations that would otherwise release fear.

With respect to the management of stress and uncertainty in busy circumstances, there will typically be an increased tendency to automatic and unreflective assessments. When operating on autopilot – and pressure of work takes over – you may be inclined to be judgemental and assessing, towards yourself as towards others. But the entailing judgements and assessments are engendered by your autopilot and a reflection of your socialised stereotypes and automated reactions. Such reactions serve the purpose of cognitive relief, but obviously come at a cost. This cost being that you will experience matters in an oversimplified way and, also, that you may propel yourself into a downward spiral.

Exercising mindfulness may offer a way out of these vicious spirals. In concrete situations, this may be a matter of your psyching up to, and allowance of, the resetting of your prejudices and assumptions in order to encounter new as old challenges with what the mindfulness literature refers to as 'beginner's mind.' This means that you will access situations with increased openness and with a more responsive (not critical or prejudiced) mind. Via a raised consciousness, you will thus avoid becoming entrapped in the *notion* of knowing what you see and feel – and your subsequent exploitation of even the most insignificant occasion for passing sentence upon a given situation.

Once, in connection with an examination at the master's education programmes, a leader said:

It's as if my brain and my narrative about myself are squeezing my heart. I can't escape. It just goes on and on, 24–7. It's weighing me down. And I'm simply so tired of being my own worst critic: I feel that I've lost all credibility – that I'm deceiving myself and my employees. I'm constantly on the move. Everything is turned over and over in my mind and, finally, becomes a veritable tyranny of thought existing inside my head. I'm so embarrassed about this, embarrassed about neither being able to – nor having the guts to – get off this self-destructive treadmill.

The practice of mindfulness can help to prevent you from getting carried away by such thoughts. Mindfulness can be applied for the development of faith in yourself and your surroundings and thus prevent you from investing unimaginable amounts of energy in controlling your surroundings. Rather, you will learn to embrace the uncertainty and non-knowledge that are characteristic of many leadership contexts of today. This practice may, moreover, contribute to your development of a much more enhanced attentiveness and presence.

A systematic practice of mindfulness will promote a non-judgemental attitude, enhanced tranquillity, and improved overview. As a mindfulness-practicing leader you will become better equipped for receiving and addressing critical thoughts – with a more open mind and with greater acceptance. Instead of experiencing considerable discomfort in connection with uncertainty and fear and struggling against these, the approach is acceptance of the emergence of uncertainty and fear. You recognise the presence of such emotions, and you are curious as to why and when they will emerge. Emotions are data carrying a message, not just disruptive elements. In situations when a leader is meeting with his/her team, and the team members are frustrated on the grounds of a decision their leader has had to announce, the emergence of emotions of uncertainty is only natural. In such circumstances, the mindfulness approach will work along the lines of opting for a curious and accepting approach to such emotions and let them be a natural companion – as opposed to evaluating oneself in negative terms, and thus let fear build up. Opting for an accommodating and accepting approach will enable a, calmer, leader to keep the meeting and him-/herself on track so as to steer the meeting to completion with his/her integrity intact.

A good approach to set about mindfulness is to locate a few good apps and then use them on a daily basis, or you can sign up for one of the eight-week courses provided practically everywhere. Another good and easy way will be to select one of your daily routines and then concretely train your mindfulness. This could be your breakfast, taking your dog out for a walk, brushing your teeth, taking the bike to work, etc. Your training must focus on being completely present in the activity you focus on, and here you need to train your attention with respect to your physical, emotional and mental activities.

Feedback

Feedback is a highly potent tool in leadership development. This applies with respect to the development of concrete collaborative relations as well as the development of the individual leader and employee and their emotional intelligence. Unfortunately, the feedback provided by organisations is negligibly small which leaves organisations with an incredibly large potential that remains untapped. One analysis (Golemann et al., 2002), performed among 177 separate surveys with participation by a total of more than 28,000 leaders, for instance showed that the more senior a leader's position in the organisational hierarchy, the less consistent feedback this leader will receive on his/her performance. If you experience that members of the senior management often appear to be callous, non-emphatic, quick on the draw, etc., this is no wonder. One particular issue in this connection is that, at these levels, leaders typically do not possess sufficient self-awareness to know about this, which has significant consequences. The same study for instance showed that executives from businesses with the poorest scores will award themselves top marks in seven out of ten leadership skills, whereas their subordinates' assessment of them is just the opposite. The effective leaders will seek out negative feedback and be open to criticism. Less effective leaders will typically seek more approving feedback. Effective leaders will typically achieve a higher accuracy in their self-awareness and performance scores (Golemann et al., 2002).

As leaders and humans, we often find it exceedingly difficult to realise how our own behaviour and style will affect our surroundings (Heen & Stone, 2014). Actually, this is not so very odd, because we never observe our own face in interaction, and likewise we never hear our own voice in interaction. But precisely our facial expression our voice constitute two decisive context markers for our audiences. They are our blind spots, albeit the hot spots to others! Blind spots will be reinforced because we, ourselves, tend to suppress our emotions, whereas to others they will count double. We will attribute our behaviour to the situation, whereas others will attribute it to our personality. We assess our own behaviour on the basis of our intentions, whereas others will assess it on the basis of the impact such behaviour will have on them.

Many leaders will refrain from seeking feedback, simply because they fear it. They are afraid to learn from peer leaders or employees that they are incompetent or that they are unpopular. For many years, we have discussed the subject of feedback with leaders, just as we have trained feedback-seeking behaviour. Many leaders actually experience that, although they have an enormous need for feedback, they consider the requesting thereof to be incredibly transcending.

In 2014, Heen and Stone wrote an amazing book on the art of receiving feedback. Based on a series of studies, this book puts the spotlight on all the inconveniences we experience to be linked with the reception of feedback. However, the authors also look into all the profits involved in feedback, for instance that feedback-seeking behaviour is related to:

- increased job satisfaction
- increased creativity at the job
- a more rapid adaptation to role or organisation
- less staff turnover
- higher performance ratings

(Heen & Stone, 2014, p. 9)

Instead of seeking real and concrete feedback, leaders will lean against organisational measurements such as job satisfaction surveys and workplace assessments which, in general, are without context and non-specific, and hence of no use relative to really investigating the matter in depth. Leaders will not get sufficient insight into, nor get anywhere near what is demanded from their leadership style, the way in which their behaviour and emotions affect the organisation, etc. This leaves many leaders in a vacuum within which they attempt to perceive and guess at what is required. And, most often, they guess wrong. We have often participated in projects, focused at designing interaction between leaders and employees, at which the leaders have been deeply mystified by the feedback coming to light.

It is almost as if it is tradition that leaders will reflect on their employees and the organisational processes, but never on themselves. It is a kind of 'round-about reflection' (Holm, 2014) where leaders will subject matters around them to considerable reflection, whereas they will completely bypass matters pertaining to themselves. Although they will reflect upon the many leadership tools available, they lack the courage to consider themselves a possible 'tool.' As an individual. They lack the courage to reflect upon their own leadership style, their disposition, their temper, and their communication.

For the past many years, much money has been invested in training people to *give* feedback – be this giraffe-language courses, assertion courses, etc. In our opinion, the majority of such courses support a basic assumption that feedback is dangerous and that people should be careful about giving it – thereby reinforcing an apprehensive feedback culture persuading us to take care and be considerate of one another.

This leads to paralysis with respect to the provision of the necessary feedback, to be received constructively.

Heen and Stone (2014) argue that we should redirect our focus – from training the *giving* of feedback, to training the *reception* of feedback. They distinguish between creating push and pull. We should move away from training people in pushing feedback towards training people in seeking it (pull). Generating pull is about being focused on the discovery and management of one's resistance to, and participation in, feedback interviews with confidence and curiosity – and without fear.

Most leaders have experienced to receive negative feedback together with the discomfort this may lead to. When we get palpitations, trembling, stomach 'cramps,' and racing thoughts, we will become unfocused, and learning will be a non-starter. We try to push away emotions, but our reactions contain important information. If we search our minds and listen to our emotions, they may perform the function of a map that can contribute to a localisation of the problems.

Heen and Stone (2014) brings attention to three typical reactions upon our reception of negative feedback:

- The truth trigger – When we experience the feedback to be untrue.
- The relation trigger – When our response to the feedback is a consequence of the person delivering it.
- The identity trigger – When we are affected on our 'self,' when our self-perception is affected, when we feel threatened, ashamed, and in a state of imbalance.

Training feedback as an element in the training of your fearless leadership is about improving your self-knowledge as well as your self-management. You have to become familiar with your reactions, and next work at coping with these reactions. Because our experience as humans is centred round our interpretations and narratives, you will, for instance, have to learn how to interpret messages and feedback. The secret is to decode these interpretations and narratives and inquire into the data behind the feedback you receive. Therefore, one method could be to ask where the feedback originates (data) and where it is going, i.e. the intentions underlying sender's feedback.

We have developed a small step-by-step guide for getting started:

1   Ask your surroundings how they experience your leadership style and how your leadership style affects their work. What does it facilitate? And how may it exert a negative influence? Make sure that you have set up a good feedback context in order that your surroundings understand why you would like their feedback, and

where there is space for giving feedback. Typically, you will practically be required to beg for getting actual feedback. Therefore, you must really be able to reason and make emphatically clear why feedback is absolutely decisive to you and your development.

2   Listen! Ask detailed questions.

3   Notice your reactions. Which of the three 'triggers' is activated?

4   Use the 1-per-cent rule: There will at least be 1 per cent of truth in the feedback you receive, however strange it may appear. In any case, the feedback will be a reflection of the reality that constitutes the basis on which the others will perceive you, and hence act.

5   Use your feedback to consider your blind spots, and to discuss these with your sparring partners. What do they think about them? Do they recognise them? What, in their opinion, should you concentrate on?

6   Reflect upon whether your 'triggers' may hide defence and fear. What is activated? And why?

7   Use action learning and mindfulness (read more about mindfulness later in this chapter) in your coping with your fear and the development of your courage.

Strategic Self-Management

It is trendy to be busy. A few years back, at a master's education programme, we experienced a leader who, during a general discussion, stated the following: "I'm not busy. I tell my middle managers that I'm not busy. I consider it to be completely out of proportion to go around saying that we are so very busy." The other leaders were flabbergasted. Imagine that he really dared to express such an opinion!

As already mentioned, the trend for leaders is to continue to increase their working hours and contribution in step with the tasks and increased complexity. Even though it is obviously with the best intentions of being even more effective, the problem is that, most frequently, this will not be the result, because the leaders get bogged down in details. Where are we going as an organisation? What are our visions and values? What does the world expect? What do our customers expecting? How is the organisational 'pulse'? How is the core task solved? Is our organisational structure the right one? Instead, leaders pant along from one meeting to the next and from task to task without assessing whether this is the most expedient use of time and resources. Leaders fail to develop their competences or their courage for strategic self-management.

Strategic self-management means having the capacity for managing oneself relative to how, what, and why work needs to be done for the purpose of generating the best possible value for one's organisation. If one is able to keep track of things, one will frequently know why it will not be wise to link oneself with this task while also accepting that specific meeting. And yet, one dares not opt out. What will people think? Will I then be in control?

These days, being a leader is often characterised by an enormous pressure, considerable workloads, minimal time, much change, etc. Management of oneself and one's workload together with the development of one's stress-management competences are thus absolutely decisive factors with respect to remaining a good, authentic leader. In order to succeed in this, you specifically need to deal with your stress: "Paradoxically, the road out of stress is to go into it … What you do not want to have any part in, you cannot change" (Holm, 2014, p. 178, authors' translation). Thus, seeking out yet a prioritising tool will not suffice! You will need to deal with the matter and work with what takes control of you when your workload puts you under pressure. Is it the fear of humiliation? Is it uncertainty? Is it the dependence on power? Is it the fear of rejection?

As a leader, you should be sure to focus on being conscious about how the extent of your workload will affect your communication, verbal as well as nonverbal. You should be conscious about your inner states and about how they affect your behaviour, and hence your surroundings. Otherwise, you risk getting out of control – or at least appear to do so: You will frequently mention how busy you are, you will often be late, you seldom keep deadlines, you make excuses when you fail to keep your promises, you will accuse others when something goes wrong, you are inattentive when others have the floor, and you often become distracted by e-mails, etc.

To get started on strategic self-management, you can:

1 form a general view of your tasks. Which tasks are most important for your contribution – in your *capacity as leader*?
2 open your calendar and analyse the latest three or four weeks. What is characteristic of your calendar? How many meetings are there? Take a critical view of your calendar. In which instances was your contribution most important? In which instances was your presence superfluous?
3 reflect upon your understanding of your role as leader. What is your leadership task? How do you ensure that tasks are carried out by your employees – and *not* by you? How will you generate results *through* your employees?
4 set aside one day a week for the purpose of providing an overview. For the purpose of reflection.
5 use your management team for discussions of status and strategy within the organisation. Set aside one or two days per quarter

for in-depth assessments, together with your team, on matters of strategy, overview and management.

6   spend time on planning your time.

Existential Self-Management

In periods of leaders' lives, they will get too far removed from their values and personally rooted intentions. This is typically owing to heavy workloads and lack of focus. Here, it may be a good idea to train the capacity for existential self-management, which is about seeking oneself in the context within which one enters; within the work relations one contributes to shape; and within the performance of the production to which one contributes (Andersen, 2013).

Most leaders tend to be really poor at caring for themselves. They are focused on the working climate of the employees: Employees must not be stressed out, and their working environment must be good. But will the leaders remember themselves? There are numerous examples of leaders who cannot withstand the pressure in the long run. Such cases will have repercussions, with consequences that will affect the entire organisation because, obviously, the leader will not have the sufficient energy to cope with the employees' working climate. And because the leader will become unfocused and fail to contribute to the shaping of the course.

According to Holmgren (2013), "Caring for oneself involves knowing oneself. Caring for others must not take precedence over caring for oneself. Caring for oneself takes priority because the relation to oneself is of ontological primacy" (authors' translation). This is comparable with a situation in an aircraft cabin when, in case of cabin pressurisation failure, you will first take on the oxygen mask, yourself, before helping your children or other people. Otherwise, you will be of no use to others. But, owing to all the tasks they need to deal with and all the meetings they must attend, the leaders have no time for caring for themselves: "But basically, what we are so busily working at getting over and done with is life itself – such as it unfolds right here and now" (Holm, 2014, p. 167, authors' translation).

Failure to look after oneself will have consequences. After the passage of some years, many leaders will experience that they have become so far removed from their values that they dare not relate to these. And this is when they fail to retain their integrity and to appear as authentic leaders.

Thus, existential self-management is also about considering one's life in a wider context. You need to consider the relations and values, in your personal life as in your work life, and to care about these. And you need to consider the relation to yourself and your own life.

On point of departure relative to the assessment of your existential self-management may be to ask yourself:

1   Are you taking proper care of yourself?
2   Are you eating too much?
3   Are you drinking too much?
4   Are you taking on too many or too few tasks?
5   Are you aiming too high?
6   Are you capable of delegating?
7   Will you lose your patience – will your hot temper run away with you?
8   Can you listen?
9   What is your opinion of your work-life balance, the balance between work and family/private life?

(Holmgren, 2013, p. 113)

Existential self-management is also about knowing one's values and own identity. What one stands for. As already mentioned, a remarkably high number of leaders will experience that their sense of identity is contrary to the predominant discourse about the leader as the confident, competent, calm, and professional leader. Hence, many leaders find it difficult to disclose their uncertainty, and they fear that they will accidentally expose it. Hay's interviews illustrate this feeling and the importance of having the courage to reveal one's uncertainty:

> I went to see one of my colleagues and said, "these are the things that I am experiencing, is it just me, am I just the stupid one?" And he said, "no, I have similar issues." And I said, "we need to do something about this, things are ridiculous, they are not working and I am going to get very frustrated and I am going to end up just jacking it in if I am not careful". And it was really interesting because it takes one person to open up and you find that lots of other people are in the same situation, but nobody wants to take that first step.

(Hay, 2014, p. 517)

Identity is not a stable phenomenon, but a fragile variable which is easily broken. We have met many a leader who, in a concrete situation, will suddenly have put his foot down. If, for instance, he was criticised by a peer leader. 'Here, I'm working my arse off – and then I have to take this from you. Have you any idea at all about how much I contribute?' As a leader, you can practice the strengthening of your courage through the development of your identity. You can do so by regularly talking about various episodes in order to get in touch with your own values. Be sure to tell peer leaders, friends, and coaches about concrete events and to examine the values you link therewith. You can seek out communities in which you can tell stories about your life in order to constantly maintain your values and story-telling muscles.

When, in our work, we focus on existential self-management, this may for instance occur in situations when leaders tend to be overly focused on conditions. When their mode of stating things reveals that they perceive themselves and their co-workers as victims of poor conditions. It may be reasonable and important to make an upwards search relative to unfair conditions and relative to successful accomplishment of one's core task. However, it sometimes happens to leaders that, in their everyday routines, they will rather grumble about the unfair conditions – if not to their employees, then to themselves. They do so in ways, however, that leave them passive. The existential philosophy (Strøier, 2013) introduces a concept describing a state in which human beings live in a state of thrownness. Indeed, there are conditions under which we live and certain relations that are given and that we cannot evade. Our body is as it is, and our health is as it is, etc. But when we refer to ourselves as being victimised in a reality over which we have no influence, we lead our lives in 'bad faith.' We deceive ourselves into avoiding the undertaking of the responsibility we have with respect to affecting our own lives and surroundings. We should rather find our freedom in our thrownness – search for own options available for action and own responsibility.

To develop your competences into existential self-management, you can:

1 speak with colleagues, friends, and coaches about your values. Your values may easily disintegrate, and your narrative muscle must be maintained on an ongoing basis.
2 keep an eye on yourself. Is my behaviour correct relative to my values as a human being?
3 continuously, reflect upon your work-life balance. Is it OK that you work so much?
4 switch off all electronic devises one hour before bedtime, and do not switch them on till one hour after you have risen. Constantly having your nose in your mobile or computer will prevent you from feeling anything at all.
5 imagine that you have contact to yourself, lying on your deathbed. You are an old and wise person. Which good advice would you give yourself, where you are now, relative to living your life?

Train Your Flexibility – Versatile Management

As mentioned in the introduction, research indicates that the leadership of the future will require mental development for the purposes of enhanced mental and behavioural flexibility. Many current leadership approaches thus focus on the necessity for leaders to adapt their leadership style to what a given situation will require, rather than one-sidedly exercising narrow leadership styles because of a biased attitude influenced by discourses or personal preferences.

Typically, leaders will not apply a sufficiently wide spectrum of leadership styles, and they tend to become too dogmatic in, and will exaggerate their application of, the leadership styles that they consider to be most natural. Typically, such preferences can be a good mix of innate personal preferences and preferences based on experiences with for instance good or bad leaders, or they can originate in leadership courses, etc. Thus, such preferences are typically applied too unilaterally. And choice of leadership style is for instance about how leaders will develop prejudices towards opposing leadership styles. A leader with a strong value with respect to involvement will typically also be prejudiced against leaders who are too controlling. And this will discourage them from training and developing such a leadership style.

Much leadership research (see e.g. Cameron et al., 2006) explicates how leaders need to succeed with a set of opposite requirements in their leadership. They must, for instance, be both supportive and capable of challenge. They must be participative as well as empowering. They must, at one and the same time, be visionary and yet keep their feet firmly planted on the ground. But, as already mentioned, many leaders risk to insist too unilaterally on one leadership style, rather than 'oscillate' in the opposite direction to a satisfactory extent. Research (see e.g. Kaplan & Kaiser, 2006; Lüscher, 2018; Cameron et al., 2006) shows flexibility in management to be of decisive importance to a leader's effectiveness. One of the most recognised leadership pipeline researchers, Rob Kaiser, has thus demonstrated that versatile management constitutes an isolated factor of 50 per cent relative to what makes up a leader's effectiveness (Kaplan & Kaiser, 2006).

Kaplan and Kaiser (2006) have developed a versatile leadership model that visualises the opposite leadership tasks and styles with which a leader must necessarily succeed.

As demonstrated in Figure 3.3, Kaplan and Kaiser distinguish between, on the one hand, competence-paired strategic *versus* operational (*what* is led); and on the other, competence-paired forcefulness *versus* opportunity enabling (*how* leadership is performed). The point

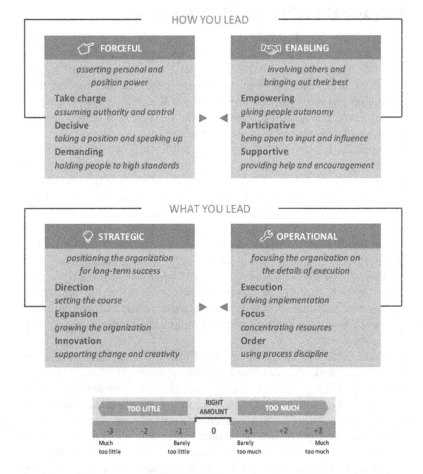

Figure 3.3 Versatile leadership model. (Kaplan & Kaiser, 2006). Copyright © 2020 by Kaiser Leadership Solutions. Used with permission.

is that to succeed as a leader, you must be able to perform flexible adaptation of your leadership relative to what a situation or process will call for. It is no good that, most frequently, you simply resort to involvement. Or always just decide on your own. On the contrary, you must be able to demonstrate flexible application of opposing competences.

Kaplan and Kaiser have demonstrated that when drawing on too few or too one-sided leadership styles, you may at the same time have a tendency to overdo your strengths. When, for years, you have not worked with the training of your flexibility, because you have insisted on and trained your preferences, your strengths have typically constituted those that have brought you where you are. But at a given point in time, you will experience that these strengths have ceased to bring you on in the world or, on the contrary, they have rendered you ineffective, because you will overdo your strengths and because you will, at the same time, become too weak with respect to your complementary strength.

Kaplan and Kaiser (2006) thus describe how leaders may underdo or overdo management styles. The leader will overdo his strength and underdo the complementary strength. Thus, a double problem will arise – partly because the leader will over-involve and partly because the leader's capacity for taking control is too feeble. To the leader, it will therefore be relevant to investigate the leadership styles applied. How is your balance relative to your extent of involvement *versus* the extent to which you give direction? What is your balance relative to the extent to which you show appreciation *versus* how hard you drive your employees? To what extent will you give people the benefit of the doubt *versus* to what extent will you hold people responsible? To what extent will you focus on the future *versus* to what extent will you focus on the 'here-and-now'? Maybe you believe that you are equally good at all elements? An interesting find in this connection is, however, that there is a consistent negative correlation: The moment you overdo one strength, this will entail a considerable risk that you will, at the same time, underdo its complementary strength.

LVI (Leadership Versatility Index) (Kaplan & Kaiser, 2006), is a leader-profile test applied for the purpose of providing an overview of leaders' leadership styles, comprising such weaknesses and strengths as are found in leaders as well as an overview of when they will be overdoing their strengths. The leaders can apply LVI as a 360-degree leadership evaluation and thus get an insight into how their surroundings perceive their strengths and weaknesses. An example of a profile is shown in Figure 3.4.

As shown by the profile, it not only uncovers weaknesses – with leaders simply failing to cultivate their leadership to a satisfactory extent, but also the overdone strengths – with leaders' too frequent application or overly usage of the same leadership style. And it further shows that, quite concretely, the two aspects are linked: the greater the tendency to overdo a strength, the greater the risk of underdoing complementary strengths.

LVI can be used in discussions with leaders concerning their preferences and the background for these. This overview will typically help leaders towards becoming curious as to the impacts of their leadership styles. The overview will constitute an opening for commencing a registration of when, by reflex reactions, leaders will be applying certain of their strengths in situations that may perhaps call for other

Figure 3.4 LVI 360-degree leadership evaluation. (Kaplan & Kaiser, 2013).
Reprinted with permission of the publisher. From *Fear Your
Strengths: What You Are Best at Could Be Your Biggest Problem.*
Copyright © 2013 by Robert E. Kaplan & Robert B. Kaiser, Berrett-
Koehler Publishers, San Francisco, CA. All rights reserved. www.
bkconnection.com.

leadership styles that they have normally refrained from using, fearing
how this will be experienced.

With respect to uncovering your strength, your overdone strength
and your weakness as well as reflection upon the backgrounds for these
circumstances, we have developed a method which takes its point of
departure in the LVI research, the human element, and immunity to
change. From the model shown in Figure 3.5, you begin by selecting the
strength you believe will best characterise you.

This is your strength. Next, you find the corresponding overdone
strength in the outer circle (Figure 3.6).

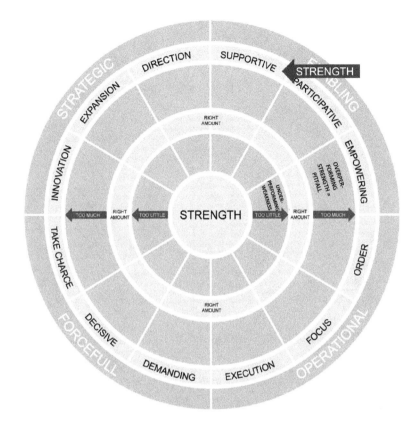

Figure 3.5 Reprinted with permission of the publisher. From F*ear Your Strengths: What You Are Best at Could Be Your Biggest Problem.* Copyright © 2013 by Robert E. Kaplan & Robert B. Kaiser, Berrett-Koehler Publishers, San Francisco, CA. All rights reserved. www. bkconnection.com.

This is your overdone strength and, to many, it will also constitute their blind spot. Next you look at the figure's opposite position. This is where you find your weakness (Figure 3.7).

This is what you should work on to establish balance in your leadership. Last, but not least, you consider the overdone strength that will complement this strength (Figure 3.8).

Here, you will typically find your prejudice, your allergy, and your fear. Prejudice, because – when you consider the strength of the circle above – what you basically fear is that your cultivation of this strength will automatically cause your aberration to the overdone strength. And this will signify your allergy. Allergy, because typically you are averse

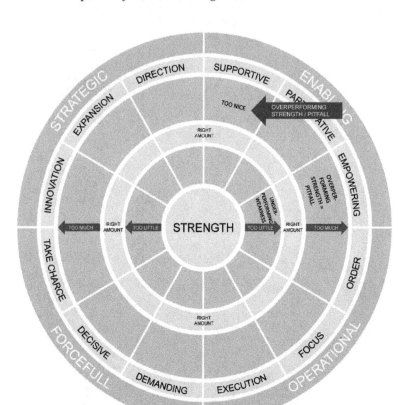

Figure 3.6 Reprinted with permission of the publisher. From *Fear Your Strengths: What You Are Best at Could Be Your Biggest Problem.* Copyright © 2013 by Robert E. Kaplan & Robert B. Kaiser, Berrett-Koehler Publishers, San Francisco, CA. All rights reserved. www. bkconnection.com.

to people following this style. Fear, because you fear that you will end up there yourself. With respect to this fear it will be a really good idea to briefly recapitulate your work on the human element (is this fear of rejection, humiliation/incompetence, or of being ignored?). Likewise, it would be a good idea to take a look at your immunity to change table and, in column three, read what worries and competing goals you have noted here. Because it can be precisely this fear that will obstruct your ability to step up your complementary strengths.

In the following you will find a list of all strengths, when overdone, and which complementary strengths you will typically not get cultivated, because you are allergic to this strength when it is overdone (Figure 3.9).

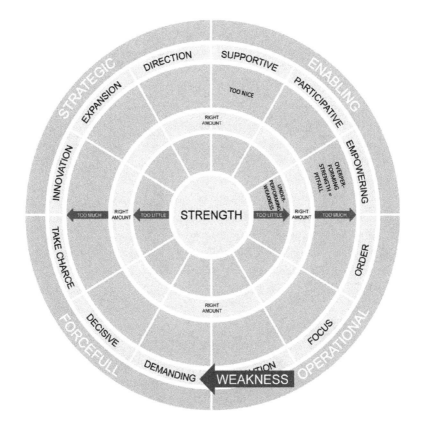

Figure 3.7 Reprinted with permission of the publisher. From *Fear Your Strengths: What You Are Best at Could Be Your Biggest Problem*. Copyright © 2013 by Robert E. Kaplan & Robert B. Kaiser, Berrett-Koehler Publishers, San Francisco, CA. All rights reserved. www. bkconnection.com.

Examples of strengths – and their imbalances – according to Kaplan and Kaiser (2013):

- Taking charge – and the imbalance: overcontrolling
- Decisive – and the imbalance: dominating at meetings
- Demanding – and the imbalance: too demanding
- Empowering – and the imbalance: showing confidence without checking
- Participative – and the imbalance: overly receptive
- Supporting – and the imbalance: too nice
- Direction – and the imbalance: no grounding

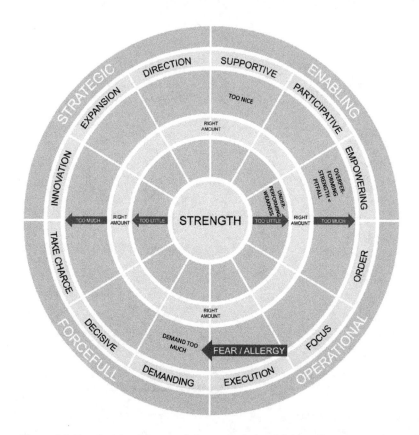

Figure 3.8 Reprinted with permission of the publisher. From *Fear Your Strengths: What You Are Best at Could Be Your Biggest Problem*. Copyright © 2013 by Robert E. Kaplan & Robert B. Kaiser, Berrett-Koehler Publishers, San Francisco, CA. All rights reserved. www. bkconnection.com.

- Expansion – and the imbalance: Bite off more than they can chew
- Innovation – and the imbalance: Fix something that already works
- Execution – and the imbalance: tunnel vision
- Focus – and the imbalance: too restrictive and cost conscious
- Order – and the imbalance: solely process-oriented

To get started on versatile management, you can:

1   Reflect upon your managerial preferences relative to leadership styles.
2   Examine the notions behind your possible inhibitions towards opposing leadership styles. By which discourses and opinions have

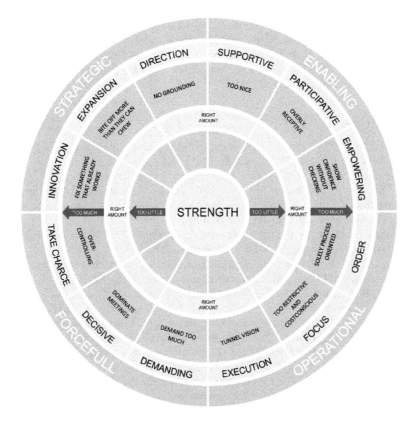

Figure 3.9 Reprinted with permission of the publisher. From *Fear Your Strengths: What You Are Best at Could Be Your Biggest Problem.* Copyright © 2013 by Robert E. Kaplan & Robert B. Kaiser, Berrett-Koehler Publishers, San Francisco, CA. All rights reserved. www. bkconnection.com.

you become entrapped? Which fear constitutes the reason behind your failure to deal with your weakness? Do you have a change immunity and what is it about?

3   Get feedback from your surroundings as to how you perform your leadership styles, your strengths, and weaknesses, and when you overdo your strengths.

4   Begin by detecting when, by reflex, you begin to apply leadership styles that you find safe, albeit they may perhaps be inexpedient in a given situation.

5   Use action learning for the purpose of training your weaknesses and adapt your leadership style to relevant situations.

Notes

1 EQ is short for emotional quotient. EQ-i 2.0 is a testing tool for measuring and assessing your emotional intelligence and social skills.
2 An app (mind of the leader) connected with the book by Hougaard (2018). *The Mind of the Leader*. Recommendable. https://apps.apple.com/us/app/the-mind-of-the-leader/id1357567241

References

Andersen, F. (2013). *Selvledelse. Selvudvikling på arbejdspladsen.* København: Dansk Psykologisk Forlag.

Bregman, P. (2013). *Why So Many Leadership Programs Ultimately Fail.* Harvard Buisness Review. https://hbr.org/2013/07/why-so-many-leadership-program

Cameron, K., et al. (2006). *Competing Values Leadership: Creating Value in Organizations.* Cheltenham: Edward Elgar.

Golemann, D., et al. (2002). *Primal Leadership: Realizing the Power of Emotional Intelligence.* Boston, MA: Harvard Business Review.

Hay, A. (2014). 'I Don't Know What I am Doing!': Surfacing Struggles of Managerial Identity Work. *Management Learning, 45*(5), 509–524.

Heen, P., & Stone, D. (2014). *Thanks for the Feedback: The Science and Art of Receiving Feedback Well.* New York, NY: Viking/The Penguin Group.

Holm, I. (2014). *Det personlige lederskab.* København: Hans Reitzels Forlag.

Holmgren, A. (2013). Ledelse med narrative og poststrukturalistiske perspektiver. In P. Helth, (ed.). *Lederskabelse – det personlige lederskab.* København: Forlaget Samfundslitteratur.

Hougaard, R. (2018). *The Mind of the Leader: How to Lead Yourself, Your People, and Your Organization for Extraordinary Results.* Boston, MA: Harvard Business Review.

Kaplan, B., & Kaiser, R. (2006). *The Versatile Leader: Make the Most of Your Strengths without Overdoing It.* San Francisco, CA: Pfeiffer/John Wiley.

Kaplan, R., & Kaiser, R. (2013). *Fear Your Strengths: What You Are Best at Could Be Your Biggest Problem.* San Francisco, CA: Berret-Koehler.

Kegan, R., & Lahey, L. (2009). *Immunity to Change: How to Overcome It and Unlock the Potential in Yourself and Your Organization.* Boston, MA: Harvard Business Review.

Lüscher, L. (2018). *Managing Leadership Paradoxes.* New York, NY: Taylor & Francis.

Stein, S., & Book, H. (2011). *The EQ Edge. Emotional intelligence and Your Success* (3rd edition). Mississauga, Ontario: John Wiley.

Strøier, V. (2013). Eksistentialisme og lederskab. In P. Helth, (ed.). *Lederskabelse – det personlige lederskab* (3rd edition). København: Forlaget Samfundslitteratur.

Conclusion

With this book, we have tried to demonstrate why courage in leadership is important. Considering the considerable complexity, pace of change, and more fluid hierarchies, and leadership roles, it is leadership that can fill the gap left by the lack of structure. Sense-making, through distinct objectives that leaders have the courage to put on the agenda, is crucial in the formation of a shared direction and collaboration. It is the base of followers of courageous, distinct, and competent leaders that will create energetic, proud, and competent organisations.

Alas, leadership courage is an article in short supply. Many leaders experience fear and uncertainty in their daily management – frequently without acknowledging how, driven by fear and uncertainty, they will: pretend to be in control of things; avoid conflict; refrain from making demands; not dare to criticise; involve to too large or too small extents; become a provider; not have the courage to take the lead and set the course.

Fear is often a matter of quite basic interhuman reactions: We fear being ignored and considered insignificant; we fear humiliation and to appear incompetent; and we fear being rejected and not being popular in the peer leader community. This fear will affect our behaviour, resulting in for instance under- or over-involvement, over- or under-control, and in our being more or less open and confidential than the situation calls for.

A series of approaches and methods may be effective in the development of yourself. To a large extent, it is about unlocking your self-awareness for the purpose of looking into why you feel as you do and how this will affect your leadership. Next you need to train, train, and train again – always being conscious about what you are training and why. The objective is for you to develop sufficient courage to use your practical judgement rather than leadership tools that refer to an instrumental rationality which is inadequate in a complex organisational working day. Practical judgement is the capability of coping with the complexity, multiplicity, and uncertainty we constantly encounter, albeit without withdrawing therefrom or making ourselves believe that we can hide behind tools. Our practical judgement is best developed through action learning whereby we competently, moment for moment, relate reflexively to our concrete experiences of what may occur in the situations within which we move, which emotions and relational dynamisms will be activated, and how we, in our capacity as leaders, will affect these in relevant ways.

Index